Let Earth Receive *Her* King

Advent, Christmas and the Kingdom of God

Jeff Doles

Let Earth Receive Her King
© 2014 by Jeff Doles. All rights reserved.

Published by
Walking Barefoot Ministries
P.O. Box 1062, Seffner, FL 33583

ISBN: 978-0-9823536-5-3

All scripture quotations, unless otherwise indicated, are from the *New King James Version*. © 1982 by Thomas Nelson, Inc. Used by permission. All rights reserved.

Scripture quotations marked *ESV* are taken from *The Holy Bible, English Standard Version*, © 2001 by Crossway Bibles, a division of Good News Publishers. Used by permission. All rights reserved.

Scripture quotations marked *HCSB* are taken from the *Holman Christian Standard Bible*®, Copyright © 1999, 2000, 2002, 2003, 2009 by Holman Bible Publishers. Used by permission. Holman Christian Standard Bible®, Holman CSB®, and HCSB® are federally registered trademarks of Holman Bible Publishers.

Scripture quotations marked *NLT* are taken from the *Holy Bible, New Living Translation*, copyright © 1996, 2004, 2007 by Tyndale House Foundation. Used by permission of Tyndale House Publishers, Inc., Carol Stream, Illinois 60188. All rights reserved.

Scripture quotations marked *NIV* are taken from *The Holy Bible, New International Version*®, NIV® Copyright © 1973, 1978, 1984, 2011 by Biblica, Inc.® Used by permission. All rights reserved worldwide.

Cover image: The Nativity, by the Cuzco School, 1725-1775. Public domain. Wikimedia Commons.

Cover design and book interior by *www.ChristianBookDesign.com*

For more resources on enjoying new life in Christ, living in faith and the power of the Holy Spirit, or to find out more about Jeff Doles, visit our websites:

www.WalkingBarefoot.com
www.TheFaithLog.com
www.JeffDoles.com

Contents

This Season of Waiting 5

Longing for Light 8

Watching in Expectation 10

Silent and Still 13

Living Between the Comings 15

Let Us Go Up to the Mountain of the LORD 17

Psalm 122 and the New Jerusalem 21

His Coming Brings Light 22

His Coming Brings Abundance and Joy 24

His Coming Brings Divine Dominion 26

A Shoot from the Stump of Jesse 29

The Spirit of the LORD Will Rest on Him 32

Gospeling in the Old Testament 36

The Genealogy of Jesus the Messiah 39

The Genealogy of the New Adam 42

The Genealogy of Deliverance 45

Joseph Pondered 48

You Shall Call His Name Salvation 50

The Greater Fulfillment Found in Messiah 53

Mary in Expectation   56

Advent of the King   59

Displacing Kings   62

The Christmas Story is Not Just for Jews   65

Shepherds' Wonder, Angels' Awe   67

The Pleasure of God   69

The Shepherds' Return   72

Simeon and Anna in Expectation   73

He Appeared in the Flesh   77

The Shekinah Dwelling (Part 1)   81

The Shekinah Dwelling (Part 2)   83

A Tabernacle for the Nations   86

Let Earth Receive Her King   89

This Season of Waiting

The season of Advent is a time of waiting and preparation. "Advent" comes from the Latin word *adventus*, which means "coming." The season of Advent is an in-between time, the time between promise and fulfillment, the time between "amen" and "there it is!" In the Church calendar, it is a time of preparation for the season of Christmas, when we will once again celebrate the birth of King Jesus.

Historically, we are waiting for something that has already come, something that has already begun. That might seem a little strange. After all, if it has already come, why do we still wait for it? But the truth is that, though it has already begun, it has not yet come in completeness. Theologians refer to this as *already, not yet*. That is, if I may make a little rhyme, we are waiting for something that is *already begun but not yet done*.

What are we waiting for? One answer comes to us in the psalms. One of my longstanding prayer habits has been to pray each day in the book of Psalms (5 psalms each day times 30 days in a month is

150 psalms—it works out nicely). One morning—a December 1st, to be precise—I was praying through Psalm 2. Since it was the season of Advent, I began to think about it in an Advent way. The psalm begins,

> *Why do the nations rage*
> *And the people plot a vain thing?*
> *The kings of the earth set themselves*
> *And the rulers take counsel together*
> *Against the LORD and against His Anointed?*
>
> *(vv. 1-2)*

Now, I had read this question many times before, but that morning I thought to ask it myself: "Lord, why do the kings of the earth *still* rage and the nations *still* plot in vain and set themselves against You and Your Messiah, Jesus?" I prayed through the psalm a little further.

> *"Yet I have set My King*
> *On My holy hill of Zion."*
> *I will declare the decree:*
> *The LORD has said to Me,*
>
> *"You are My Son,*
> *Today I have begotten You.*
> *Ask of Me, and I will give You*
> *The nations for Your inheritance,*
> *And the ends of the earth for Your possession."*
>
> *(vv. 6-8)*

Yahweh says, "Yet I have set My King on My holy hill of Zion." Past tense, completed action. This was the enthronement of a freshly anointed king over Israel. The New Testament attributes this psalm to David, who said, "I will declare the decree." God had given David a decree and this was what He said to him: "You are My son, today I have begotten you." In the ear of an ancient Israelite, this was the language of adoption. When God made David king, He "adopted" him as His son. This psalm, then, applied to David. But by extension, it also applied to all those of his royal lineage who would ascend to his throne.

But there is also a much deeper and prophetic significance at work here. Neither David nor his descendants saw the fulfillment of the promise. None saw the nations for their inheritance and the ends of the earth for their possession. Indeed, before long the throne of David began to crumble and the divided kingdom of Israel and Judah eventually entered into a long exile, a deep time of waiting for a Messiah who was yet to come and for a kingdom that would endure.

Finally, after long centuries, a new light finally began to dawn: The birth of Jesus, Son of David, who came announcing that the time was fulfilled and God's kingdom had now come. The most important thing in the world was happening.

- At the Incarnation, when Jesus came and took upon Himself our humanity.
- At the Cross, when He took upon Himself our sin and destroyed the works of the devil.
- At the Resurrection, when He took upon Himself our mortality and defeated it.
- At the Ascension, when He assumed His place at the right hand of the Father, where He now rules and reigns over all.

And yet … we are still waiting for the completion of what was begun. Ever since the days of John the Baptist, the kingdom of God has been "forcefully advancing" (Matthew 11:12 *NIV*). Still we wait. "The darkness is passing away and the true light is already shining" (1 John 2:8). Still we wait. We pray the prayer Jesus taught us to pray, "Kingdom of God, come. Will of God, be done on earth as it is in heaven" (my paraphrase). And still we wait for the day He comes again and receives all the nations for His inheritance and the ends of the earth for His possession. That will be the greatest Advent.

Longing for Light

LORD, lift up the light of Your countenance upon us. (Psalm 4:6)

David cries out to God in this psalm. He is in distress.

Hear me when I call, O God of my righteousness!
You have relieved me in my distress;
Have mercy on me, and hear my prayer.

(Psalm 4:1)

God has brought him relief before in times of distress. Now he needs divine relief again. "Hear me ... have mercy on me ... hear my prayer," he petitions. This is what troubles him now (v. 2):

How long, O you sons of men,
Will you turn my glory to shame?
How long will you love worthlessness
And seek falsehood?

David is beset by people who take everything that is good and turn it into shame, who love and value what is worthless and honor what is false. "How long?" he asks. Here, he addresses his opponents directly, but elsewhere in the Psalms he directs the question to God: "How long, O LORD?" (See Psalm 6:3; 13:1-2; 35:17; 74:10; 89:46; 94:3-4).

Not to make a pun here, but David is *longing*. That is one of the things that captures me in this psalm during Advent season. Advent is not only a time of waiting and preparing, it is a season of yearning. Yet, though David longs, he is not in despair. Though he yearns, he is not without hope. Indeed, he is drawn by the expectation that God will free him from his afflictions once again. "The LORD will hear when I call to Him" is his confidence (v. 3).

David is not the only one going through this. His people are experiencing the same troubles. "Who will show us any good?" they ask (v. 6). David gives the answer in the second half of the verse as he turns their question into prayer: "LORD, lift up the light of Your countenance upon *us*."

This is another thing that captures my Advent imagination: Light—the light that comes from God. Though the darkness seems to be closing in all around, David knows who the source of light is: Yahweh, the God with whom David and his people are in covenant.

You have put gladness in my heart,
More than in the season that their grain and wine increased.
I will both lie down in peace, and sleep;
For You alone, O LORD, make me dwell in safety.

(vv. 7-8)

David began in distress but now he is glad, lighthearted. He has turned it over to God and is longing toward the Lord, longing for the light of God. The answer has not yet turned up but he knows that it will. He rests in *shalom*, the divine peace and wholeness that comes from God. His trust is in Yahweh, who alone settles him in safety.

Longing and light. As we sit in the Advent shadows, surrounded by many distressing things that threaten our world, we watch, we wait, and we yearn for the light that comes from the Lord alone. Only He can make us dwell in safety. And He will.

Watching in Expectation

Give ear to my words, O LORD,
Consider my meditation.
Give heed to the voice of my cry,
My King and my God,
For to You I will pray.
My voice You shall hear in the morning, O LORD;
In the morning I will direct it to You,
And I will look up.

(Psalm 5:1-2)

David has spoken his words and thought his thoughts to the Lord. He has cried out to his King. He has brought his request, and brought it early, before God. He has directed his heart toward God, casting his cares on Him. There is now only one thing left to do: "And I will look up." The *NIV* says, "And wait in expectation;" the *HSCB*, "And watch expectantly." It is the essence of hope.

Today, we often use our English word "hope" in a tentative or speculative way, to speak of things we *desire* to happen, things that *can* happen and perhaps *will* happen. Perhaps, or perhaps not. But that is not how the Bible uses the Hebrew and Greek words for "hope." They speak of a positive expectation, a joyful anticipation. There is a confidence to them. "Faith is the substance of things hoped for, the evidence of things not seen" (Hebrews 11:1). The word for "substance" is about the assurance and underlying reality of what is hoped for. Faith, then, is the underlying reality of things we do not yet see but fully expect to come to pass.

So, David brings his meditation—his "sighing" (*HCSB*)—before God, and now he has hope. But why? What is the reason for his renewed expectation?

> *For You are not a God who takes pleasure in wickedness,*
> *Nor shall evil dwell with You.*
> *The boastful shall not stand in Your sight;*
> *You hate all workers of iniquity.*
> *You shall destroy those who speak falsehood;*
> *The* LORD *abhors the bloodthirsty and deceitful man.*
>
> *(vv. 4-6)*

David is confident because he knows that God is not pleased by wickedness, nor with those who take pleasure in wickedness. The proud, the boastful, the bloodthirsty, the deceitful—these were the kinds of people who were troubling David, the kinds of people who are still in the world today! God is not happy with them. They do not honor His way or believe His Word. They have no faith, and without faith, it is impossible to please God. But David follows a different path.

> *But as for me, I will come into Your house in the multitude*
> *of Your mercy;*

> *In fear of You I will worship toward Your holy temple.*
> *Lead me, O LORD, in Your righteousness because of my enemies;*
> *Make Your way straight before my face.*
>
> *(vv. 7-8)*

David leans hard into the one who has revealed Himself in covenant relationship by the name *Yahweh* (rendered in English by the word *LORD*, in small caps). It is the name by which God has promised to be steadfast in love and mercy toward His people. The righteousness of Yahweh is not just His goodness in general. It is, more particularly, the *faithfulness* of God in keeping His covenant. What God has promised, He will do. David comes depending on God's covenant love and faithfulness. There is no faithfulness in David's enemies, only falseness and flattery. They are wicked to the core and full of destruction, their throats like open tombs and their words like snares (v. 9).

David is waiting now, but for what is he watching? For God to come and settle the issue, to set things right and hold his enemies accountable. It is time for their counsels to fail, for them to fall by their own plans and to be put out of the community so that they can no longer trouble the innocent and the good. For in coming against God's covenant people, they have rebelled against God Himself (v. 10). That is not the extent of David's expectation, though. He also has a joyful anticipation concerning the covenant people themselves—his expectation is for them, too.

> *But let all those rejoice who put their trust in You;*
> *Let them ever shout for joy, because You defend them;*
> *Let those also who love Your name*
> *Be joyful in You.*
> *For You, O LORD, will bless the righteous;*

> *With favor You surround him as with a shield.*
>
> *(vv. 11-12)*

God honors those who honor Him, and keeps covenant with those who keep covenant with Him. He shows Himself faithful to those who keep faith with Him. He fills them with His joy and surrounds them with His favor.

Advent is a season of waiting and watching. Though there are many troubles all around, and we are living in between the *already* of God's kingdom breaking into the world and the *not yet* of when it comes in completeness, God fills us with His joy and surrounds us with His favor. So we look up in joyful anticipation of what God is going to do next and how King Jesus will set everything right.

Silent and Still

> *My soul, wait silently for God alone,*
> *For my expectation is from Him.*
>
> *(Psalm 62:5)*

Once again, David has come before the Lord. He waits silently before God. It is not that he is settled in the midst of calm. Quite the opposite. He is surrounded, once again, by those who seek his downfall, false friends who pretend to bless him while inwardly cursing him (vv. 3-4).

But David comes quietly before God. It does not happen naturally. He has to remind his soul, perhaps even repeating it over and over to himself, instructing himself: "Soul! Wait silently for God alone."

"Wait silently" translates one word, not two. The waiting implies silence and the silence implies patience. But it also speaks of stillness. David is not probing his heart for some desperate plan to deal with these pretenders on his own. No, he has instructed his heart to sit quietly and still before God alone. Nothing else will do. Only God can help him.

"For my expectation is from Him." Some versions translate this as "For my *hope* is from Him." In the Bible, hope *is* expectation. What is especially interesting here is that David says, "My expectation is *from* Him." Not *in* but *from*, as if to add a layer of specificity. David does not have just a general hope in God, or that things will somehow turn out okay. No, he expects something particular from God, for God to move specifically on his behalf. He has a personal relationship with God, so his expectation is for God's personal attention. The hope that David has comes *from* God.

He alone is my rock and my salvation,
My stronghold; I will not be shaken.
My salvation and glory depend on God;
My strong rock, my refuge, is in God.

(vv. 6-7)

Though surrounded by disloyalty and deceit, David stills his heart before God. The longer he remains in that inner quiet, the more he realizes how much he needs God, but also how much God is for him. Now the assurance rises up in him: He will not be shaken. His position is secure, for God really is his strong rock of refuge. Now he turns to those who have remained loyal to him, and who are disquieted by the dangers that have threatened him—and them.

Trust in Him at all times, you people;
Pour out your hearts before Him.
God is our refuge.

Selah.

The world does not slow down, nations do not cease their striving, nor do obligations go away while we quiet out hearts before God. We must quiet them anyway, reminding our souls that our expectation is from God alone, that He is our rescue and refuge, and that our glory—every good thing in our lives—comes from Him. It is in that realization that we come to know that whatever is happening in the world cannot shake us, for we are not founded on the world but on upon God.

Though the world does not know what to do with it, Advent is a season for quieting our hearts and setting our expectation on God. For He comes, as He did so many centuries ago and has done so many times since, bringing His salvation and releasing His glory. In the quiet of Advent, our hearts are refreshed as we wait for expectation to be fulfilled anew.

Living Between the Comings

When the LORD brought back the captivity of Zion,
We were like those who dream.
Then our mouth was filled with laughter,
And our tongue with singing.
Then they said among the nations,
"The LORD has done great things for them."

> The LORD has done great things for us,
> And we are glad.
>
> Bring back our captivity, O LORD,
> As the streams in the South.
> Those who sow in tears
> Shall reap in joy.
> He who continually goes forth weeping,
> Bearing seed for sowing,
> Shall doubtless come again with rejoicing,
> Bringing his sheaves with him.
>
> *(Psalm 126)*

The psalm writer is thinking about when Israel first began to return from Babylonian captivity. It was a wonderful time, like a dream full of laughter and joy. It was a God thing. But he also realizes that there is still more that needs to be done—there are still others in captivity, and even those who have already been freed are still under the dominion of foreign kings. He is living between the "comings," between the first release from captivity and the final fulfillment when all the captives come home. And that means there is still much sowing to be done and also much more reaping. There are still many tears yet to be shed, but also much rejoicing to follow, for the greater harvest is yet to come.

Like the psalm writer, we too are living between the "comings." Between the *first* coming of King Jesus into the world to establish the kingdom of God and the *second* coming when He will return and the kingdom of God will fill all the earth. In between, however, the kingdom increases and multiplies, like a mustard seed that a man sows in his garden. It is a small seed, yet when it is sown it becomes a large tree where many birds can nest in its branches (Luke 13:18-19). Again, the kingdom is like leaven that a woman works into a large batch of flour. It is a small amount, yet when it is activated and released into the dough, it grows and multiplies until it permeates the whole lump and changes it completely (Luke 13:20-21).

Jesus taught the disciples to pray to the Father, "Your kingdom, come. Your will, be done on earth as it is in heaven" (my paraphrase). And His kingdom *has* come, and His will has *already* begun to be done on earth as it is in heaven. But it has not yet come in all its fullness, so we keep praying. And watching. And sowing.

King Jesus has come into the world. He lived and died and rose again. Now He is ascended to the throne of God at the right hand of the Father, the place of ruling and reigning. When He returns, there will be a great rejoicing and the harvest will be complete. Meanwhile, we live between the "comings."

Let Us Go Up to the Mountain of the Lord

Advent means "coming." In ancient Rome, the *adventus* was a ceremony in honor of the emperor, welcoming him into the city, often as he returned from a victorious military campaign. The Christian season of Advent is a time of waiting and preparation that focuses on the arrival of Jesus the Messiah, God's Anointed King, into the world. This was His *first* coming, and we remember it as Christmas. But in this season we also have an eye toward His *second* coming, when He will return at the end of the age.

At His first coming, the kingdom of God came into the world and the promises of God began to be fulfilled. At His second coming, the kingdom and all those promises will be brought to completion. In the season of Advent, we remember these promises as we prepare to celebrate the birth of King Jesus, but also as we await the return of the King.

God has much to say about these promises. Isaiah long ago prophesied what would come in the "last days." We often think of this as the "end times," and envision the robed and bearded man, all cartoon-like, walking the city with a sign announcing, "Repent! The end is near!" But here in Isaiah, the "last days" are about the completion of God's plan, the fulfillment of all He has promised His people. The first anticipation of hope Isaiah brings is found in chapter 2:

In the last days
The mountain of the LORD's house will be established
At the top of the mountains
And will be raised above the hills.
All nations will stream to it,
And many peoples will come and say,

> *"Come, let us go up to the mountain of the LORD,*
> *To the house of the God of Jacob.*
> *He will teach us about His ways*
> *So that we may walk in His paths."*

For instruction will go out of Zion
And the word of the LORD from Jerusalem.
He will settle disputes among the nations
And provide arbitration for many peoples.
They will turn their swords into plows
And their spears into pruning knives.
Nations will not take up the sword against other nations,
And they will never again train for war.

House of Jacob, come and let us walk in the LORD's light.

(Isaiah 2:2-5 HCSB)

This foretells a time when God will reign over all the nations of the earth, from His holy city, Zion. They will all come to His holy mountain, to the house of the Lord, His temple, the place where He dwells on earth. From there He will send forth His Word into all the world and disciple the nations in His ways. The Lord will judge between the nations and set everything right. There will be no more need for the implements of war—there will be no more war.

This began to be fulfilled when Jesus was born in Bethlehem. The Word, who is God, became flesh and "dwelt" (literally, "tabernacled") among us (John 1:14). God became present with us as a human being through Jesus the God-Man, who is fully human as well as fully divine.

After resurrection and before He ascended to His throne in heaven at the right hand of the Father, Jesus gathered His disciples and declared: "All authority has been given to me in heaven and on earth" (Matthew 28:18). Then He commissioned them to go out into the world:

Go therefore and make disciples of all the nations, baptizing them in the name of the Father and of the Son and of the Holy Spirit, teaching them to observe all things that I have commanded you; and lo, I am with you always, even to the end of the age. (Matthew 28:19-20)

You shall receive power when the Holy Spirit has come upon you; and you shall be witnesses to Me in Jerusalem, and in all Judea and Samaria, and to the end of the earth. (Acts 1:8)

This is the instruction of the Lord going forth from Zion, His word from Jerusalem to all the nations. At the end of the book of

Revelation, we see God's holy city, the New Jerusalem, coming down and joining heaven to earth.

> Then one of the seven angels who had the seven bowls filled with the seven last plagues came to me and talked with me, saying, "Come, I will show you the bride, the Lamb's wife." And he carried me away in the Spirit to a great and high mountain, and showed me the great city, the holy Jerusalem, descending out of heaven from God ...
>
> But I saw no temple in it, for the Lord God Almighty and the Lamb are its temple. The city had no need of the sun or of the moon to shine in it, for the glory of God illuminated it. The Lamb is its light. And the nations of those who are saved shall walk in its light, and the kings of the earth bring their glory and honor into it. Its gates shall not be shut at all by day (there shall be no night there). And they shall bring the glory and the honor of the nations into it ...
>
> And he showed me a pure river of water of life, clear as crystal, proceeding from the throne of God and of the Lamb. In the middle of its street, and on either side of the river, was the tree of life, which bore twelve fruits, each tree yielding its fruit every month. The leaves of the tree were for the healing of the nations. (Revelation 21:9-10, 22-26; 2:1-2)

Here is the mountain of the Lord, the Holy City and the Temple where God dwells forever with His people. It is the kingdom of God come into the world, the will of God being done on earth exactly as it is being done in heaven. Here are all the nations of the world bringing all their glory to honor King Jesus the Lamb. And here they all find their healing and restoration at the Tree of Life.

At Advent, we prepare our hearts to celebrate the coming of the Lord Jesus into the world at Bethlehem two thousand years ago. We do this even as we live in the present reality of His Lordship and watch for His future coming—and the fulfillment of all things. Let us go up to the mountain of the Lord and walk in His light.

Psalm 122 and the New Jerusalem

An Advent adaptation of Psalm 122 in light of Isaiah 2:2-5, Revelation 21 and the coming of King Jesus into the world:

I was light and bright and full of joy
When they came and said to me,
"Let us go up to the house of Yahweh."
Our feet shall stand within your gates, O Jerusalem,
The city of God come down
From heaven to earth.

It is a city built together,
Joining heaven and earth as one:
Where the tribes go up,
The tribes of Yahweh,
To fulfill the testimony of Israel,
And give thanks to the name of Yahweh.

For there He will set things right among the nations.
From the throne of the house of David,
Where King Jesus, the Anointed one,
Rules and reigns forever.

Pray for the peace of the New Jerusalem:
"They shall prosper who love you.
Shalom be within your walls,
And prosperity within your palaces.

For the sake of my brothers and sisters,
For the sake of the nations,
I will say, even now, 'Peace be with you.'
Because of the house of Yahweh our God
I will seek your good."

Let us go up to the mountain of the Lord and walk in His light.

His Coming Brings Light

The people who walked in darkness
Have seen a great light;
Those who dwelt in a land of deep darkness,
On them has light shined.

(Isaiah 9:2 ESV)

Isaiah 9 is a messianic prophecy. That is, it foretells the coming of Messiah into the world. Verse 1 speaks of the judgment the northern tribes of Israel experienced because of their rebellion against God. But there was also a promise of a time of future restoration:

But there will be no gloom for her who was in anguish. In the former time he brought into contempt the land of Zebulun and the land of

Naphtali, but in the latter time he has made glorious the way of the sea, the land beyond the Jordan, Galilee of the nations. (Isaiah 9:1 ESV)

Zebulun was in the lower portion of Galilee and Naphtali in the upper, but both were overshadowed, oppressed by the Syrians and Phoenicians and corrupted by their ways. The "way of the sea" was the region of the Sea of Galilee. The name "Galilee" comes from a Hebrew word that means "circle." Zebulun and Naphtali were surrounded, encircled by the nations in upper Galilee.

The promise was that the light of Yahweh would once again break through the darkness and shine brightly in this region. After the long night, a new dawn would come. Matthew finds this new dawn in the ministry of Jesus. However, it was not just the dawning of Jesus' ministry, but the kingdom of God itself arising in the earth, and it was present in the person of the King.

Now when Jesus heard that John had been put in prison, He departed to Galilee. And leaving Nazareth, He came and dwelt in Capernaum, which is by the sea, in the regions of Zebulun and Naphtali, that it might be fulfilled which was spoken by Isaiah the prophet, saying:

The land of Zebulun and the land of Naphtali,
By the way of the sea, beyond the Jordan,
Galilee of the Gentiles:
The people who sat in darkness have seen a great light,
And upon those who sat in the region and shadow of death
Light has dawned.

From that time Jesus began to preach and to say, "Repent, for the kingdom of heaven is at hand." (Matthew 4:12-17)

Years before, an old man named Simeon had been watching for this light and this kingdom, for he had received a promise from God that he would see it in his lifetime. On the day Mary and Joseph brought the baby Jesus for dedication in the Temple, the Spirit of God led Simeon in also. When he saw the child, he took Him up in his arms and praised God:

> *Lord, now You are letting Your servant depart in peace,*
> *According to Your word;*
> *For my eyes have seen Your salvation*
> *Which You have prepared before the face of all peoples,*
> *A light to bring revelation to the Gentiles,*
> *And the glory of Your people Israel."*
>
> (Luke 2:29-32)

The coming of King Jesus the Messiah into the world brings a light that reveals the glory of God to all the nations of the earth.

His Coming Brings Abundance and Joy

> *You have multiplied the nation;*
> *You have increased its joy;*
> *They rejoice before you*
> *As with joy at the harvest,*
> *As they are glad when they divide the spoil.*
>
> (Isaiah 9:3 ESV)

In Isaiah 9, the prophet has slipped into prophetic poetry. It was not the song the people in his own day were singing but one that would arise in the northern and southern territory of Galilee. It is cast in a prophetic tense, singing it as though it were already accomplished. In this way, Isaiah demonstrates the assurance that it would come to pass.

The Hebrew word for "multiplied" means increase, abundance, expansion, enlargement, to become great and many. Israel, the people of the promise given to Abraham, would multiply and increase in number and influence because of the Light that would dawn in Galilee. But there would also be an increase in joy, like that of harvest time. The time of sowing in tears past, the time of reaping and gathering begun. A festival time. And gladness, like that of dividing the spoils. Ecstatic joy! The Hebrew word for "gladness" here literally means to turn about or spin around. Why such exuberance? Because the enemy has been broken and what was stolen has been restored, with plenty more besides. See how the prophet sings in verses 4-5:

> *For the yoke of his burden,*
> *And the staff for his shoulder,*
> *The rod of his oppressor,*
> *You have broken as on the day of Midian.*
> *For every boot of the tramping warrior in battle tumult*
> *And every garment rolled in blood*
> *Will be burned as fuel for the fire.*
>
> *(ESV)*

The lifting of the burden, the breaking of the yoke, deliverance from the oppressor—this is the work of the Anointed One, of Messiah! It is fulfilled in the coming of King Jesus. There is a similar prophecy later in Isaiah, and the Gospel of Luke records how Jesus took it as the charter of His ministry. Jesus was just beginning His ministry when He was asked to stand in the synagogue and read from the Scriptures. He opened the scroll to the prophecy in Isaiah 61:

> *The Spirit of the Lord is upon Me,*
> *Because He has anointed Me*
> *To preach the gospel to the poor;*
> *He has sent Me to heal the brokenhearted,*
> *To proclaim liberty to the captives*
> *And recovery of sight to the blind,*
> *To set at liberty those who are oppressed;*
> *To proclaim the acceptable year of the Lord.*

Then sitting down to teach, Jesus declared, "Today this Scripture is fulfilled in your hearing" (see Luke 4:17-22). It was the kingdom of God breaking into the world. Not all at once or in all its fullness, mind you, but as a seed, yet one that has been growing and expanding ever since.

All of this, as the prophet foretold in Isaiah 9:1-2, would begin in Galilee, in the circle of the nations. It would be not only for Israel's benefit but for all the nations on earth. For the coming of King Jesus the Messiah into the world brings abundance of blessing and ecstatic joy for all who trust in Him.

His Coming Brings Divine Dominion

> *For unto us a Child is born,*
> *Unto us a Son is given;*
> *And the government will be upon His shoulder.*

*And His name will be called
Wonderful, Counselor, Mighty God,
Everlasting Father, Prince of Peace.*

(Isaiah 9:6 ESV)

We continue in the prophetic song in Isaiah 9. So far, Isaiah has spoken of the dawn of a great light in the midst of darkness, the enlargement of the nation of Israel, ecstatic joy like that of the harvest and of portioning out the spoils of victorious battle. He has sung of the yoke being shattered, the burden being destroyed and the rod of the oppressor being broken.

But how would all this come about? Isaiah reveals the surprising answer: "For unto us a *Child* is born, unto us a Son is given." The dawning of the light comes in the birth of a child. Not just any child, but one that is given by God. This is the Anointed Son ultimately meant by King David's prophecy in Psalm 2:

*"Yet I have set My King
On My holy hill of Zion."
I will declare the decree:
The LORD has said to me,*

*"You are My Son,
Today I have begotten You.
Ask of Me, and I will give You
The nations for Your inheritance,
And the ends of the earth for Your possession.
You shall break them with a rod of iron;
You shall dash them to pieces like a potter's vessel."*

(Psalm 2:6-9)

It is this Messiah King of which Isaiah now sings. The government will rest upon His shoulders and to Him will be given dominion—a kingdom. He is called by a series of titles, all of which emphasize His divinity.

- *Wonderful.* The Hebrew word refers to miracles that distinguish Him from all others and inspire wonder. Messiah would not only *work* wonders but would Himself *be* a wonder.
- *Counselor.* This speaks of great wisdom and purpose, and the ability to guide His people with divine counsel.
- *Mighty God.* This name indicates divine power and strength. Messiah does not come as one who is merely *like* God but as one who *is* God, as this name indicates elsewhere in Scripture (see Jeremiah 32:8 and especially, because it is so close in context, Isaiah 10:21).
- *Everlasting Father*, or Father of Eternity. As such, He will not decline and fade away, as other kings must, but will rule and reign forever.
- *Prince of Peace.* His reign is one that brings divine peace (Hebrew, *shalom*). This is prosperity and wholeness in every way.

Isaiah now turns our attention to the *kingdom* of this eternal King.

Of the increase of his government and of peace
There will be no end,
On the throne of David and over his kingdom,
To establish it and to uphold it
With justice and with righteousness
From this time forth and forevermore.
The zeal of the LORD of hosts will do this.
(Isaiah 9:7 ESV)

The reign of God's Messiah King will increase until His glory is revealed in all the earth, and every nation of the world will experience the peace and prosperity of His dominion. This was God's plan in choosing Abraham in the first place, and of making of Him a great nation. And this was His purpose in choosing David—a "man after His own heart," as the prophet Samuel said (1 Samuel 13:14)—to be its king.

This divine plan is now in the process of being fulfilled in the reign of King Jesus, son of David and son of Abraham, to redeem humanity, restore all of creation and accomplish the mandate God gave Adam to "be fruitful and multiply," to "fill the earth and subdue it," and to "have dominion" (Genesis 1:28). He is now establishing and enlarging His kingdom throughout the earth. It is a kingdom of justice and rightness that will last forever.

Though it has not yet come in all its fullness, this kingdom is already breaking into the world and will be complete when the King comes again. Just as Jesus first entered the world as a child but then grew up into His destiny, likewise, His kingdom starts small but continues to grow until it will one day fill the earth. The zeal of the LORD of Hosts, which is the intense desire and purpose of God, will bring it through to completeness. For the coming of King Jesus the Messiah brings the dominion of God into all the world.

A Shoot from the Stump of Jesse

The tree had been felled and all hope had been dashed. The kingdom that once was had now been broken in two. God's promise to David, the son of Jesse, of an heir who would reign forever, had apparently failed. But wait! What's this? There is still life in the old stump.

All is not lost and there is still hope, for a new shoot has emerged.

*Then a shoot will grow from the stump of Jesse,
And a branch from his roots will bear fruit.*

(Isaiah 11:1 HCSB)

The tree was the Davidic kingdom of Israel, which had been divided into two, Israel and Judah, after Solomon, David's son, died. Israel, the northern kingdom, was about to be carried off into captivity by Assyria (Isaiah 8). However, a remnant of Israel would return from exile—but only a remnant—and they would turn to the LORD in faith (Isaiah 10:20*ff*). Then, Isaiah promised, the burden of the oppressor would be lifted off their shoulders and the yoke would be destroyed from off their neck (Isaiah 10:27). The power of the enemy would be completely shattered. And now Isaiah foretells a shoot that would grow from the stump of Jesse.

A remnant and a shoot. That seems so little and so small. And yet, that is very often how God does His work. Indeed, in another place God says, "Do not despise these small beginnings" (Zechariah 4:10 *NLT*). In the book of Daniel, the prophet interprets the dream of Nebuchadnezzar and speaks of the Messiah who would come in like a small stone but would "grow" to become a great mountain that fills the whole earth. He would break in pieces the other kingdoms and establish a kingdom that would stand forever—the kingdom of God (see Daniel 2:29-45).

This is a prophecy of Messiah. The Lord Jesus is the "stone" that smashes all the other kingdoms and becomes a great "mountain" that fills the whole earth. He began His ministry in Galilee, preaching the gospel of God's kingdom, "The time is fulfilled and the kingdom of God is at hand" (Mark 1:14-15). At the cross, He disarmed the principalities and powers, which are the demonic influences behind all the kings and cultures of the world (Colossians 2:15). He established the kingdom of heaven on earth, which has been growing and increasing ever since. Remember how Jesus described the kingdom in the parables He taught.

- "The kingdom of God is as if a man should scatter seed on the ground, and should sleep by night and rise by day, and the seed should sprout and grow, he himself does not know how." (Mark 4:26)
- "What is the kingdom of God like? And to what shall I compare it? It is like a mustard seed, which a man took and put in his garden; and it grew and became a large tree, and the birds of the air nested in its branches." (Luke 13:18-19)
- "To what shall I liken the kingdom of God? It is like leaven, which a woman took and hid in three measures of meal till it was all leavened." (Luke 13:20-21)
- "From the days of John the Baptist until now, the kingdom of heaven has been forcefully advancing, and forceful men lay hold of it" (Matthew 11:12 *NIV*).

The kingdom of God starts small but grows big. Even the Messiah, the Word who "became flesh and dwelt among us" (John 1:14), had a small beginning in the world. Born in a tiny, inconspicuous town, nestled in the insignificance of an old feeding trough, visited by shepherds and star geeks. And yet, this is the one of whom Isaiah prophesied,

For unto us a Child is born,
Unto us a Son is given;
And the government will be upon His shoulder.

And His name will be called
Wonderful, Counselor, Mighty God,
Everlasting Father, Prince of Peace.
Of the increase of His government and peace
There will be no end,
Upon the throne of David and over His kingdom,
To order it and establish it with judgment and justice
From that time forward, even forever.
(Isaiah 9:6-7)

Messiah came into the world as a child, an infant, a tiny shoot from an old sawed-off stump. But He is the promised Son of David, and He grew up to sit on the throne of David, where He rules and reigns forever. His kingdom has come and is bearing fruit, and it will keep on increasing and advancing until it fills the whole earth.

The Spirit of the LORD Will Rest on Him

The Spirit of the LORD will rest on Him,
The Spirit of wisdom and of understanding,
The Spirit of counsel and of might,
The Spirit of the knowledge and the fear of the LORD.
(Isaiah 11:2 NIV)

The promise of God in Isaiah 11:1 was that a shoot would come forth from the stump of Jesse, a strong branch that would bear fruit. In verse 2, we learn that the Spirit of the LORD would be upon Him, a sign of His divine authority and dominion. These are the attributes of the one who reveals God's kingship in the world:

- ❧ *The Spirit of wisdom and of understanding* is skill, prudence, insight, and discernment of what is of right and wrong, true and false, effective and ineffective.
- ❧ *The Spirit of counsel and of might* is about purpose and the power to fulfill it, the strategy and strength to prevail.
- ❧ *The Spirit of the knowledge and fear of the* LORD is intimate fellowship with God, being pleasing to Him in all things.

Now see how this plays out and what it means in the world.

His delight is in the fear of the LORD,
And He shall not judge by the sight of His eyes,
Nor decide by the hearing of His ears;
But with righteousness He shall judge the poor,
And decide with equity for the meek of the earth.
He shall strike the earth with the rod of His mouth,
And with the breath of His lips He shall slay the wicked.
Righteousness shall be the belt of His loins,
And faithfulness the belt of His waist.
(Isaiah 11:3-5)

Messiah is all about the "fear on the Lord" and totally focused on pleasing God. He came to do the Father's will, not His own. He does not judge, He does not act, He does not speak according to outward appearances or even out of His own desire.

Most assuredly, I say to you, the Son can do nothing of Himself, but what He sees the Father do; for whatever He does, the Son also does

> *in like manner ... I can of Myself do nothing. As I hear, I judge; and My judgment is righteous, because I do not seek My own will but the will of the Father who sent Me. (John 5:19, 30)*

> *I do nothing of Myself; but as My Father taught Me, I speak these things. And He who sent Me is with Me. The Father has not left Me alone, for I always do those things that please Him. (John 8:28-29)*

> *For I have not spoken on My own authority; but the Father who sent Me gave Me a command, what I should say and what I should speak ... Therefore, whatever I speak, just as the Father has told Me, so I speak. (John 12:49-50)*

Therefore, His verdict is impartial, for God does not look upon the outward appearance but upon the heart. Messiah adjudicates fairly, according to what is right and does not side with the oppressor against the poor, as so many kings of Isaiah's day had done (and have done since). He deals with all with an even hand. He judges the wicked of the land by the word of His mouth—the Word of God—and they will be no more. He sets things right by His faithfulness, and the result of His righteous rule will be peace throughout the earth, which is painted here in terms of idyllic splendor.

> *The wolf also shall dwell with the lamb,*
> *The leopard shall lie down with the young goat,*
> *The calf and the young lion and the fatling together;*
> *And a little child shall lead them.*
> *The cow and the bear shall graze;*
> *Their young ones shall lie down together;*
> *And the lion shall eat straw like the ox.*

The nursing child shall play by the cobra's hole,
And the weaned child shall put his hand in the viper's den.
They shall not hurt nor destroy in all My holy mountain,
For the earth shall be full of the knowledge of the LORD
As the waters cover the sea.
(Isaiah 11:6-9)

The peaceableness of Messiah's kingdom will prevail, transforming even creation itself. "For the earnest expectation of the creation," Paul says, "eagerly waits for the revealing of the sons of God. For the creation was subjected to futility, not willingly, but because of Him who subjected it in hope; because the creation itself also will be delivered from the bondage of corruption into the glorious liberty of the children of God" (Romans 8:19-21).

And in that day there shall be a Root of Jesse,
Who shall stand as a banner to the people;
For the Gentiles shall seek Him,
And His resting place shall be glorious.
(Isaiah 11:10)

Messiah has become a banner, a gathering point for His people, who He is calling to return from exile. Even the Gentiles (the nations) come seeking Him. Paul quotes this verse from Isaiah near the end of his letter to the Jesus followers at Rome: "And again, Isaiah says: 'There shall be a Root of Jesse; and He who shall rise to reign over the Gentiles, in Him the Gentiles shall hope'" (Romans 15:12).

The nations will come to Him willingly, not by coercion, but in expectation, trusting Him. They will bow before Him and confess Him as Lord of all. His "resting place," the place where He dwells in the midst of His people, and from which He rules and reigns, will display the greatness of His glory.

> *Therefore God also has highly exalted Him and given Him the name which is above every name, that at the name of Jesus every knee should bow, of those in heaven, and of those on earth, and of those under the earth, and that every tongue should confess that Jesus Christ is Lord, to the glory of God the Father. (Philippians 2:9-11)*

Gospeling in the Old Testament

Advent is all about the gospel, the coming of God's Messiah, and His kingdom, into the world. The gospel is the announcement of that King and that kingdom.

What does gospeling—the preaching of the gospel—look like in the Old Testament? The Greek word for "gospel" is *euaggelion* which means "good news." Associated with it is the word *euaggelizo*, from which we get the word "evangelize" and which means to "announce good news." In the Septuagint (or LXX, the ancient Greek translation of the Old Testament), we find the word *euaggelizo* a number of times.

- It is used to announce the defeat of an enemy (1 Samuel 31:9; 2 Samuel 4:10; 2 Samuel 18:19-31).
- It is used to proclaim great victory. In Psalm 68, which extols the victory of Yahweh over the enemies of His people, we read, "The LORD gave the word; great was the company of those who *proclaimed* it" (v. 11).
- It is used to proclaim God's righteousness, His faithful acts in

delivering His people: "I have *told the glad news* of deliverance in the great congregation; behold, I have not restrained my lips, as you know, O LORD. I have not hidden your deliverance within my heart; I have spoken of your faithfulness and your salvation; I have not concealed your steadfast love and your faithfulness from the great congregation" (Psalm 40:9-10 *ESV*).

- In Psalm 96, it is used to speak of God's saving acts for His people and to declare His glory to the nations: "Sing to the LORD, bless His name; *proclaim the good news* of His salvation from day to day. Declare His glory among the nations, His wonders among all peoples" (Psalm 96:2-3).

- Isaiah 40, a Messianic passage, speaks of the coming of the LORD to shepherd His people and rule over their enemies: "O Zion, you who *bring good tidings*, get up into the high mountain; O Jerusalem, you who *bring good tidings*, lift up your voice with strength, lift it up, be not afraid; say to the cities of Judah, 'Behold your God!'" (v. 9).

- In Isaiah 52, another Messianic passage, it is used to announce the peace (*shalom*, wholeness) and salvation that comes from God, and to proclaim His reign: "How beautiful upon the mountains are the feet of him who *brings good news*, who proclaims peace, who *brings glad tidings* of good things, who proclaims salvation, who says to Zion, 'Your God reigns!'" (v. 7).

- In Isaiah 60, still in Messianic mode, it is used of all the nations coming to proclaim the praises of Yahweh. "A multitude of camels will cover you, the young camels of Midian and Ephah; all those from Sheba will come; they will bring gold and frankincense, and will *bear good news* of the praises of the LORD" (v. 6 *NASB*).

- In Isaiah 61, it is used in regard to the anointing of the Messiah. "The Spirit of the Lord GOD is upon Me, because the LORD has anointed Me to *preach good tidings* to the poor; He has sent Me to heal the brokenhearted, to proclaim liberty to the captives, and the opening of the prison to those who are bound. To proclaim the acceptable year of the LORD." The whole chapter speaks of God's Anointed King coming to set everything right in the world. It is this entire passage that Jesus indicated when He quoted the first verses and then declared, "Today this Scripture is fulfilled in your hearing" (Luke 4:17-21).

- In Jeremiah 20:15, *euaggelizo* is used to announce the birth of a child.

- In Joel 2:32, it relates back to the promise in Isaiah 40:9 about good news coming out of Zion and Jerusalem. "And it shall come to pass that whosoever shall call on the name of the Lord shall be saved: for in mount Zion and in Jerusalem shall the saved one be as the Lord has said, and they that have *glad tidings preached* to them, whom the Lord has called" (*Brenton's English Septuagint*).

- In Nahum 1:15, it speaks of the deliverance of God's people from their enemies. "Behold, on the mountains the feet of him who *brings good tidings*, who *proclaims* peace! O Judah, keep your appointed feasts, perform your vows. For the wicked one shall no more pass through you; he is utterly cut off." (A similar word, *apaggelizo*, is here translated "proclaims.")

The use of *euaggelizo* in the Septuagint is significant because the Septuagint was the Bible for the early Church. Whenever the New Testament writers quote from the Old Testament, most often it is from a version of the Septuagint. So the early Church was familiar with what *euaggelizo* and *euaggelion* conveyed.

The gospeling we find in the New Testament fits very well with the gospeling we find the in the Old Testament. All its categories find their ultimate fulfillment in Jesus the Messiah. He is the One whose birth was announced when angels brought "good tidings" (*euaggelizo*) to the shepherds in the field (Luke 2:10-11). He is the King whose kingdom the gospel proclaims (e.g., Mark 1:14-15). He is the Anointed One who fulfills the gospel in Isaiah 61. He is the Good Shepherd who brings His people peace (John 10:11, John 14:27). He is the one who has destroyed the works of the devil (1 John 3:18) and disarmed the "principalities and powers" (Colossians 2:15). Not only has He won the victory over the enemy, but through Him we also are "more than conquerors" (Romans 8:37). The gospel of the kingdom of God is all about Jesus the King.

The Genealogy of Jesus the Messiah

Matthew begins his telling of the gospel with a long list of who begat who, from Abraham to David, and finally, to Jesus. It is a record of waiting—waiting for Messiah. It began with God's promise to Abraham, which was confirmed to his son Isaac, then again to Isaac's son Jacob. The promise was that, through their descendants, God would bless all the nations and families of the earth. Generation after generation lived in that expectation, though they did not know exactly how it would come about. So, Matthew opens with a genealogy that has an important story to tell us. Even the very first sentence is loaded with revelation.

> *The book of the genealogy of Jesus the Messiah, the Son of David, the Son of Abraham. (Matthew 1:1)*

The mere fact that there is a genealogy at all tells us something significant: Jesus did not appear on the scene from out of nowhere, from some distant land, nor did He drop down from heaven to begin a brand new story. No, He came as part of an old, old story, one stretching back generation after generation, back through David, back to Abraham, and through Abraham, all the way back to the beginning.

Nor was Jesus merely the latest installment in that story. Rather, He came as the Messiah (or "Christ," which means the same thing) and, as such, as the one in whom that old, old story finds it fulfillment. God had long promised, through Moses and the prophets, that one would come who was Anointed (which is what "Messiah" and "Christ" mean) and who would not only deliver His own people, the nation of Israel, but would be king over *all* the nations of the earth. He would set everything right that was wrong in the world. Matthew makes it clear, right from the beginning, that Jesus is that Messiah.

The story of which Jesus is the fulfillment is not only a very old story, it is also a very big one, big enough for the whole world. Although Matthew could have gone all the way back and begun his genealogy with Adam, he begins with Abraham.

Abraham was a pagan whose father was an idol maker and served others gods. God called Abraham to leave his father's house and family and go to a place that God would show him (Genesis 12:1). God made him a promise: "I will make you a great nation; I will bless you and make your name great; and you shall be a blessing. I will bless those who bless you, and I will curse him who curses you; and in you all the families of the earth shall be blessed" (Genesis 12:2-3).

God was not out to bless Abraham and His physical descendants alone, but His plan was to bless *all* the families of the earth through Abraham. The apostle Paul picks up on this in his letter to the Jesus followers in Galatia: "Christ has redeemed us from the curse of the law, having become a curse for us ... that the blessing of Abraham might come upon the Gentiles in Christ Jesus, that we might receive the promise of the Spirit through faith" (Galatians 3:13-14).

Jesus the Messiah is the Son of Abraham through whom that promise is fulfilled. He is also the Son of David. For God had also made a marvelous promise to David, that He would make David's house great and establish his throne forever.

> *When your days are fulfilled and you rest with your fathers, I will set up your seed after you, who will come from your body, and I will establish his kingdom. He shall build a house for My name, and I will establish the throne of his kingdom forever ... And your house and your kingdom shall be established forever before you. Your throne shall be established forever.* (2 Samuel 7:12-13, 16)

> *I have made a covenant with My chosen,*
> *I have sworn to My servant David:*
> *"Your seed I will establish forever,*
> *And build up your throne to all generations."*
>
> (Psalm 89:3-4)

> *The LORD has sworn in truth to David;*
> *He will not turn from it:*
> *"I will set upon your throne the fruit of your body.*
> *If your sons will keep My covenant*
> *And My testimony which I shall teach them,*
> *Their sons also shall sit upon your throne forevermore."*

For the Lord has chosen Zion;
He has desired it for His dwelling place:
"This is My resting place forever;
Here I will dwell, for I have desired it.
I will abundantly bless her provision;
I will satisfy her poor with bread.
I will also clothe her priests with salvation,
And her saints shall shout aloud for joy.
There I will make the horn of David grow;
I will prepare a lamp for My Anointed.
His enemies I will clothe with shame,
But upon Himself His crown shall flourish."
(Psalm 132:11-18)

Jesus the Messiah is that Son of David, the Anointed One who perfectly fulfills the covenant and testimony of the Lord. In Him, the throne of David is established forever, with salvation, joy, strength and prosperity for all who belong to Him.

In this very first verse of his gospel account, then, Matthew draws up the history of Israel, along with the wonderful covenant promises God made to Abraham and David, and announces that it is all fulfilled in Jesus, the Anointed One.

The Genealogy of the New Adam

Matthew begins his telling of the Gospel with this: "The book of the genealogy of Jesus the Messiah, the Son of David, the Son of Abraham" (Matthew 1:1). We have already looked at the significance of Abraham and David in this lineage, but there is also another interesting feature in this verse, particularly in the way it begins: "The book of the genealogy."

The Greek words rendered as "book of the genealogy" is *biblos geneseos*. It is very reminiscent of another genealogy, the one given in Genesis about Adam: "This is the book of the genealogy of Adam" (Genesis 5:1). In the Septuagint, the ancient Greek translation of the Hebrew Scriptures, Genesis 5:1 has the same phrase Matthew used, *biblos geneseos*. Though there are a number of other genealogies in the Old Testament, we find this Greek phrase only here, in Genesis 5—and then again in Matthew 1:1, which turned out to be the first verse of the New Testament.

There is something important going on here. Matthew parallels the genealogy of Jesus the Messiah with that of Adam. The apostle Paul, in his letters to the Jesus followers at Rome and Corinth, makes explicit comparison between Adam and Jesus. He states that Adam "is a type of Him who was to come," and shows that what was lost to us through the rebellion of Adam has been won back to us, and in greater measure, through the obedience of Jesus (Romans 5:14-21).

The difference between Adam and Jesus is the difference between death and life. In 1 Corinthians 15, Paul again compares Adam and Jesus: "For as in Adam all die, even so in Christ all shall be made alive" (v. 22). "And so it is written, 'The first man Adam became a living being.' The last Adam became a life-giving spirit" (v. 45). Then Paul drills down further.

> *The first man was of the earth, made of dust; the second Man is the Lord from heaven. As was the man of dust, so also are those who are made of dust; and as is the heavenly Man, so also are those who are heavenly. And as we have borne the image of the man of dust, we shall also bear the image of the heavenly Man. (1 Corinthians 15:47-49)*

The life in view here is not just spiritual in nature but physical as well. In First Corinthians 15, Paul tells us about the resurrection of Jesus bodily from the dead and what that means in regard to our own coming resurrection. The contrast between the man of earth and the Lord from heaven is not that the Lord comes to carry our bodiless spirits off to heaven, far, far away. Rather, the point is that Jesus has come to bring heaven to earth, that we may bear His image and live in His resurrection in the world He created, now and forever.

> *Now this I say, brethren, that flesh and blood cannot inherit the kingdom of God; nor does corruption inherit incorruption. Behold, I tell you a mystery: We shall not all sleep, but we shall all be changed—in a moment, in the twinkling of an eye, at the last trumpet. For the trumpet will sound, and the dead will be raised incorruptible, and we shall be changed. For this corruptible must put on incorruption, and this mortal must put on immortality. (1 Corinthians 15:50-53)*

The kingdom of God is heaven come to earth. It is the will of God being done on earth as it is in heaven. The gospel is about the kingdom of God, and Jesus came preaching it: "The time is fulfilled, and the kingdom of God is at hand. Repent, and believe in the gospel" (Mark 1:14-15). Though it has not yet arrived in all its fullness—and will not until King Jesus returns—it has already begun. Our bodies, however, are frail and subject to death (which is what is indicated by "flesh and blood"), and if we are to be a part of God's eternal kingdom of heaven on earth, they bodies must be changed. Not put off, mind you, but changed—made incorruptible, immortal.

This is new creation. It was described prophetically in the Old Testament, and King Jesus declared it in the New, saying, "Behold, I make all things new" (Revelation 21:5). It has already begun in the

Advent, Christmas and the Kingdom of God

resurrection of Jesus from the dead, which is the firstfruits of the new creation and the guarantee of our own coming resurrection from the dead. All who receive King Jesus the Messiah are already part of this new creation. "Therefore, if anyone is in Christ, he is a new creation; old things have passed away; behold, all things have become new" (2 Corinthians 5:17). Even now, the power of God that raised Jesus from the dead is at work in us (Romans 8:11, Galatians 2:20, Ephesians 1:19-20 and Ephesians 3:20—let the marvelous truth of these passages sink in). All creation itself is waiting for this, that it may be "delivered from the bondage of corruption into the glorious freedom of the children of God" (Romans 8:19-21).

Adam was the first man of the old creation—Jesus is the first Man of the new! His coming into the world not only fulfills the story of Israel that began in Abraham, and not only fulfills the promises God made to David, but it goes back all the way to the beginning, to Adam. In Jesus, the New Adam, what was lost to the first Adam is now being restored and, indeed, all creation will be made new.

The Genealogy of Deliverance

Matthew lays out the genealogy of Jesus the Messiah in three sets of fourteen generations. In this way, he highlights Abraham and David—we have already looked at their significance in Israel's story and the story of Jesus—but he also draws attention to something else: Jewish captivity in Babylon.

> *So all the generations from Abraham to David are fourteen generations, from David until the captivity in Babylon are fourteen generations, and*

from the captivity in Babylon until the Christ are fourteen generations. (Matthew 1:17)

The kingdom of Israel was divided in 922 BC, soon after the death of King David's son, Solomon. Both kingdoms eventually proved to be unfaithful to God, breaking covenant with Him and following after false gods. The northern kingdom, Israel, fell to the Assyrians and began to be carried off into exile in about 740 BC. From 597 to about 586 BC, the Babylonians conquered the southern kingdom of Judah, capturing the city of Jerusalem, destroying the temple and deporting the inhabitants. This captivity lasted for about 70 years, after which the people were allowed to begin returning to Judea, though many chose to remain in Babylon.

However, even though the Jews were returned to the land and were even allowed to rebuild Jerusalem and the temple, they were still held captive by a series of foreign powers that were hostile to them and their God. But God promised that there would one day be a deliverer, the Messiah, who would come and conquer all His enemies and lead His people into freedom and prosperity. The prophet Ezekiel, writing during the first years of the Babylonian captivity, delivers this powerful promise from the Lord, quoted here at length:

> *Therefore say to the house of Israel, 'Thus says the Lord GOD: "I do not do this for your sake, O house of Israel, but for My holy name's sake, which you have profaned among the nations wherever you went. And I will sanctify My great name, which has been profaned among the nations, which you have profaned in their midst; and the nations shall know that I am the LORD," says the Lord GOD, "when I am hallowed in you before their eyes. For I will take you from among the nations, gather you out of all countries, and bring you into your own land. Then I will sprinkle clean water on you, and you shall be*

clean; I will cleanse you from all your filthiness and from all your idols. I will give you a new heart and put a new spirit within you; I will take the heart of stone out of your flesh and give you a heart of flesh. I will put My Spirit within you and cause you to walk in My statutes, and you will keep My judgments and do them. Then you shall dwell in the land that I gave to your fathers; you shall be My people, and I will be your God. I will deliver you from all your uncleannesses. I will call for the grain and multiply it, and bring no famine upon you. And I will multiply the fruit of your trees and the increase of your fields, so that you need never again bear the reproach of famine among the nations. Then you will remember your evil ways and your deeds that were not good; and you will loathe yourselves in your own sight, for your iniquities and your abominations. Not for your sake do I do this," says the Lord GOD, "let it be known to you. Be ashamed and confounded for your own ways, O house of Israel!"

'Thus says the Lord GOD: "On the day that I cleanse you from all your iniquities, I will also enable you to dwell in the cities, and the ruins shall be rebuilt. The desolate land shall be tilled instead of lying desolate in the sight of all who pass by. So they will say, 'This land that was desolate has become like the garden of Eden; and the wasted, desolate, and ruined cities are now fortified and inhabited.' Then the nations which are left all around you shall know that I, the LORD, have rebuilt the ruined places and planted what was desolate. I, the LORD, have spoken it, and I will do it."

'Thus says the Lord God: "I will also let the house of Israel inquire of Me to do this for them: I will increase their men like a flock. Like a flock offered as holy sacrifices, like the flock at Jerusalem on its feast days, so shall the ruined cities be filled with flocks of men. Then they shall know that I am the LORD."' (Ezekiel 36:22-38)

This was the messianic age that the Jews looked forward to, an unprecedented time of peace and prosperity. God promised to cleanse them of their unfaithfulness and put a new heart and a new spirit—God's own Spirit—within them. And all the nations would give testimony to Yahweh, the God of Israel. The prophet Jeremiah, writing just before the captivity, brings a similar message in Jeremiah 31:23-40, saying that Yahweh would make a new covenant with the house of Israel and the house of Judah. This covenant would not be like the one they broke but one that God Himself would write on their hearts (vv. 31-33). This covenant would never be broken because it would be God's own Spirit fulfilling it in them.

The Babylonian captivity, so carefully highlighted for us by Matthew, reminds us of that dark time and the grimness of the captivity that still remained for the Jews. More than that, however, it puts us in mind of the promise God made of a Deliverer who would come for Israel. This promise is fulfilled in the coming of King Jesus the Messiah into the world.

Joseph Pondered

Now the birth of Jesus Christ was as follows: After His mother Mary was betrothed to Joseph, before they came together, she was found with child of the Holy Spirit. Then Joseph her husband, being a just man, and not wanting to make her a public example, was minded to put her away secretly. But while he thought about these things, behold, an angel of the Lord appeared to him in a dream. (Matthew 1:18-20)

In Luke's telling of the Christmas story, when the shepherds came running and found the baby Jesus and revealed what the angels had announced to them in the field, Mary "pondered" all these things in her heart (Luke 2:19). In Matthew's account, we learn that Joseph had some pondering of his own, but a pondering of a very different sort.

Joseph was "betrothed" to Mary. Legally, it was more binding than what we would today call an "engagement," but they were not yet living together as husband and wife, as the marriage had not yet been consummated. Then one day, while he was making his plans and preparations, Joseph suddenly learned some very disturbing news: Mary was pregnant—and Joseph knew he was not the father.

Joseph was shattered. The life he was preparing would now not take place. His dream was irreparably broken. He turned the matter over and over in his thoughts, his head in hard tension with his heart. He was bewildered. Had Mary betrayed him? It certainly seemed that way to him—he had not yet come to understand that the child she carried inside her was of the Holy Spirit.

Now he considered what he must do. The choice before him was not whether to continue the marriage. It was a foregone conclusion that he would not—could not. The only decision was whether he would allow Mary to be subjected to public disgrace. But he was a "just man," Matthew tells us, a man who understood something about covenant love, and he was not willing for her to be openly shamed. So he would divorce her quietly. Just sign the papers and walk away. But while he was pondering these things, he had a dream. An angel of the Lord came to him and said,

> *Joseph, son of David, do not be afraid to take to you Mary your wife, for that which is conceived in her is of the Holy Spirit. And she will bring forth a Son, and you shall call His name JESUS, for He will save His people from their sins.*

> *So all this was done that it might be fulfilled which was spoken by the Lord through the prophet, saying: "Behold, the virgin shall be with child, and bear a son, and they shall call his name Immanuel," which is translated, "God with us." (Matthew 1:20-23)*

Joseph woke up and did as the angel of the Lord told him. He took Mary as his wife, just as he had planned. But everything was different now, but that would be okay. Because now he realized that this was part of a much bigger plan. Not his own plan, but God's, and that was a plan that meant great healing and forgiveness for his people. Mary gave birth to a son, and Joseph called his name *Jesus*. He was "God with us" in a new and supremely redemptive way.

And that was something for Joseph to ponder the rest of his life.

You Shall Call His Name *Salvation*

The angel of the Lord appeared to Joseph in a dream and told him not to be afraid to take Mary as his wife, for the child she carried was conceived of the Holy Spirit. "And she will bring forth a Son, and you shall call His name JESUS, for He will save His people from their sins" (Matthew 1:21).

The connection between the name of Jesus and what it means is not apparent in our English translations. Even the explanatory comment in this verse does not explain much for us in English. "Jesus" is how the name comes over to us from the Greek name "Iesous." In turn, "Iesous" was the Greek rendering for the Hebrew name "Yeshua," and it is the Hebrew name that we want to focus on here, because even in Greek, the explanatory comment is not very helpful.

So the angel said, "You shall call His name *Yeshua*, for He will save His people from their sins," but the connection is still not clear. We need to remember, however, that the angel did not speak to Joseph in English. Joseph probably did know Greek as a matter of his occupation. He was a "carpenter," a builder, perhaps a stone mason, who was probably involved in the building projects at nearby Sepphoris, which was a prosperous city for commerce, and where Greek came in very handy. But Greek was not Joseph's primary language. He was a Jew in Judea, so his first language was Hebrew, or more likely its cousin, Aramaic.

In Hebrew, the word for "save" is *yasha*. The various forms of this word appear over 300 times in the Old Testament and almost every instance refers to the saving acts of Yahweh, the salvation that comes from the LORD. The noun related to *yasha* is *yeshuah*, which means "salvation." As a personal name, *yeshuah* becomes *Yeshua*. So the name of Jesus means "Salvation." What the angel was saying to Joseph was, "You shall call His name Salvation (*Yeshua*), for He will save (*yasha*) His people from their sins."

And now the connection is clear. But what does it mean that *Yeshua* will save His people from their sins? First, notice that this concerns *His people*, which was Israel, and remember that one of the divisions Matthew presents in the genealogy of Jesus has to do with the Babylonian captivity. "So all the generations from Abraham to David are fourteen generations, from David until the captivity in Babylon are fourteen generations, and from the captivity in Babylon until the Christ are fourteen generations" (Matthew 1:17).

Israel was sent into exile, scattered among the nations, because they had defiled the land by their bloodshed and idolatry, and profaned the name of the Lord (see Ezekiel 36:17-21). But God promised that He would make His name holy among the nations. "'And I will sanctify

My great name, which has been profaned among the nations, which you have profaned in their midst; and the nations shall know that I am the Lord,' says the Lord God, 'when I am hallowed in you before their eyes'" (Ezekiel 36:23). He would do this by delivering Israel, and here is how it would be:

> *For I will take you from among the nations, gather you out of all countries, and bring you into your own land. Then I will sprinkle clean water on you, and you shall be clean; I will cleanse you from all your filthiness and from all your idols. I will give you a new heart and put a new spirit within you; I will take the heart of stone out of your flesh and give you a heart of flesh. I will put My Spirit within you and cause you to walk in My statutes, and you will keep My judgments and do them. Then you shall dwell in the land that I gave to your fathers; you shall be My people, and I will be your God. (Ezekiel 36:24-28)*

God promised He would cleanse Israel from all her filthiness and idolatry, by which she had defiled the land and profaned the name of the Lord. In other words, He would *save her from her sins*. What is more, He would give her a new heart and put His own Spirit within her (think here of Pentecost, in Acts 2), so that she would walk in His ways. And so Israel would be restored.

The Son born of Mary would be called Yeshua—Salvation!—because He would *save His people from their sins*. What was immediately in view here was Israel, Jesus' own people. But as we see from the Ezekiel passage, by this salvation the Lord would cause His name to be sanctified among the nations. The salvation Jesus brought to Israel would become salvation for the whole world, and indeed, at the end of the book of Matthew, we find the disciples being sent out to declare King Jesus to the nations (Matthew 28:18-20).

The Greater Fulfillment Found in Messiah

The Gospel According to Matthew makes it clear that the child Mary carried was conceived not by any man but by the Spirit of God. "Now the birth of Jesus Christ was as follows: After His mother Mary was betrothed to Joseph, before they came together, she was found with child of the Holy Spirit" (Matthew 1:18). The angel of the Lord told Joseph, "Do not be afraid to take to you Mary your wife, for that which is conceived in her is of the Holy Spirit" (v. 20). Matthew sees in this the fulfillment of a prophetic word spoken by Isaiah some 700 years earlier.

> *So all this was done that it might be fulfilled which was spoken by the Lord through the prophet, saying: "Behold, the virgin shall be with child, and bear a Son, and they shall call His name Immanuel," which is translated, "God with us." (Matthew 1:22-23, quoting Isaiah 7:14)*

This word from Isaiah is something of a mystery. It was given in response to a particular historical moment within Isaiah's own day. Many Bible scholars agree that it had a meaning pertaining to that time, but as with many of the signs and events of the Old Testament, it also seemed to have a significance larger than its own time. Alfred Edersheim comments on how Jews tended to view Old Testament writings:

> *Perhaps the most valuable element in Rabbinic commentation on Messianic times is that in which, as so frequently, it is explained, that*

> *all the miracles and deliverances of Israel's past would be re-enacted, only in a much wider manner, in the days of the Messiah. Thus the whole past was symbolic, and typical of the future. It is in this sense that we would understand the two sayings of the Talmud: "All the prophets prophesied only the days of the Messiah" (Sanh. 99a), and "The world was created only for the Messiah" (Sanh. 98b). (The Life and Times of Jesus the Messiah)*

We can see how this played out in the ministry of Jesus. On the day the Lord was raised from the dead, He encountered two disciples who were on their way to Emmaus. They had not recognized Him and He had not revealed His identity to them, but He spoke to them about the meaning of Messiah: "And beginning at Moses and all the Prophets, He expounded to them in all the Scriptures the things concerning Himself" (Luke 24:27). This was not merely a matter of citing an explicit prophecy here and there about Messiah. But the whole of the Old Testament continually pushes toward the coming of the messianic age, the coming of God's rule and reign over Israel and the nations, the coming of God's kingdom—and God's King—into the world.

Isaiah's prophesy about the virgin, whatever else it may have meant for its own day, appears to speak beyond its own time and with a greater meaning. In the immediate context, Isaiah gives the word to King Ahaz, but he addresses it to the "house of David" (Isaiah 7:13), in this way perhaps enlarging this prophecy with messianic significance, for Messiah would be the Son of David. This enlargement would be quite in line with the messianic theme that is woven throughout the rest of the book of Isaiah.

However, saying that this prophecy had a greater messianic meaning does not explain how it would actually work out in history. There does not appear to have been any expectation among the Jews that their Messiah would be conceived by the Holy Spirit. Would they have even been able to imagine such a thing? Some things are better grasped in retrospect—but isn't that how God works so very often? He is able to do "exceedingly abundantly above all that we ask or think," Paul tells us (Ephesians 3:20). God comes and arranges things and answers prayers and fulfills promises in ways that may be very different, and much better, than we might have expected or could have ever imagined.

So here is how Messiah came into the world, conceived not by any man but by God Himself, through the Holy Spirit, and born of the Virgin Mary. Now that it had happened in that way, Matthew could see how it fit in with the ancient prophecy, unexpectedly and in a way much greater than could have been imagined. It also gave greater significance to the prophetic statement, "They shall call His name Immanuel."

Immanuel means "God with us." In Isaiah's day, they could easily have understood that as God watching over His people, hearing and delivering them with mighty acts of divine providence. God certainly is with us in that sense. But to see what actually happened, that the Messiah was conceived by the Spirit of God, that He was actually divine as well as human ... well, that raises the meaning of *Immanuel* to new and unexpected heights: God really is with us—in Person!

Now, the name actually given to this child was Jesus, not Immanuel. Yet He is spoken of as Immanuel, "God with us," because that is actually what He is. John, in his telling of the gospel, brings out this same truth but in quite a different way. In John 1:1, he speaks of Jesus as the Word and identifies Him as God. Then in verse 14, he declares, "The Word became flesh and dwelt among us." This was the God of heaven making His abode with humanity on earth, and in a much greater way than was ever expected.

Mary in Expectation

Behold the maidservant of the Lord! Let it be to me according to your word. (Luke 1:38)

The angel Gabriel spoke the promise to Mary, "Do not be afraid, Mary, for you have found favor with God. And behold, you will conceive in your womb and bring forth a Son, and shall call His name Jesus. He will be great, and will be called the Son of the Highest; and the Lord God will give Him the throne of His father David. And He will reign over the house of Jacob forever, and of His kingdom there will be no end" (Luke 1:30-33).

Mary did not doubt, but she did not understand. "How can this be, since I do not know a man?" she asked (v. 34). So the angel told her. Now, the promise was amazing enough, but the explanation was even more astonishing: "The Holy Spirit will come upon you, and the power of the Highest will overshadow you; therefore, also, that Holy One who is to be born will be called the Son of God. Now indeed, Elizabeth your relative has also conceived a son in her old age; and this is now the sixth month for her who was called barren. For with God nothing will be impossible." (vv. 35-37).

The favor of God had truly come upon Mary. And her response was simple and direct: "Behold the maidservant of the Lord! Let it be to me according to your word." The word of the Lord had come, and Mary presented herself to God and thus laid hold of His promise. Her expectation was now set: Whatever the angel of God had spoken, that is what would come to pass. The Holy Spirit would come upon her and she would bear the Son of God, who would assume the throne of David and bring God's eternal kingdom into the world.

As the Child began to grow inside her, so did Mary's expectation of what God's word to her meant. Pregnant and pondering, she visited her cousin Elizabeth, who was well beyond childbearing years but was also herself miraculously with child, who would be known as John the Baptist. When Mary entered the house, Elizabeth's babe quickened inside her and she immediately recognized the significance, for the angel Gabriel had also come to her husband, Zachariah, with the promise of a child who would be "filled with the Holy Spirit, even from his mother's womb. And he will turn the children of Israel to the Lord their God" (Luke 1:15-16).

So, Elizabeth, too, was living in divine expectation, and now the child in her womb was alerting her that the Lord had come to her home. Filled with the Holy Spirit, she said, "Blessed are you among women, and blessed is the fruit of your womb! But why is this granted to me, that the mother of my Lord should come to me? For indeed, as soon as the voice of your greeting sounded in my ears, the babe leaped in my womb for joy. Blessed is she who believed, for there will be a fulfillment of those things which were told her from the Lord" (Luke vv. 42-45). Elizabeth's expectation had increased, and it now included expectation for the promise that had been given to Mary. At this, Mary poured out her all her ponderings in a magnificent song of praise.

> *My soul magnifies the Lord,*
> *And my spirit has rejoiced in God my Savior.*
> *For He has regarded the lowly state of His maidservant;*
> *For behold, henceforth all generations will call me blessed.*
> *For He who is mighty has done great things for me,*
> *And holy is His name.*

> *And His mercy is on those who fear Him*
> *From generation to generation.*
> *He has shown strength with His arm;*
> *He has scattered the proud in the imagination of their hearts.*
> *He has put down the mighty from their thrones,*
> *And exalted the lowly.*
> *He has filled the hungry with good things,*
> *And the rich He has sent away empty.*
> *He has helped His servant Israel,*
> *In remembrance of His mercy,*
> *As He spoke to our fathers,*
> *To Abraham and to his seed forever.*
>
> (Luke 1:46-55)

See how big her expectation. It was not just about what God was doing for *her*, but what He was doing for *Israel* and, more than that, how He was fulfilling the word He spoke to Abraham. This was the promise that He would bless all the families of the world through the seed of Abraham. Mary's expectation was as big as the world. Even though she had not yet given birth to Jesus, she counted God's promise to Abraham as fulfilled. For whatever God has begun, He will bring to completion—and God had truly begun something divine in Mary.

Advent is a season of great expectation. A season for believing the fulfillment of all that God has promised. A season for presenting ourselves to the Lord and saying, "Behold the servant of the Lord! Let it be to me according to your word."

Advent of the King

He will be great, and will be called the Son of the Highest; and the Lord God will give Him the throne of His father David. And He will reign over the house of Jacob forever, and of His kingdom there will be no end. (Luke 1:32-33)

A throne and a kingdom signify a King. The birth of Jesus, His coming into the world, is the fulfillment of the promise God made long ago to David, that his descendent would forever occupy his throne. Isaiah likewise prophesied concerning the birth of this King.

For unto us a Child is born,
Unto us a Son is given;
And the government will be upon His shoulder.
And His name will be called
Wonderful, Counselor, Mighty God,
Everlasting Father, Prince of Peace.
Of the increase of His government and peace
There will be no end,
Upon the throne of David and over His kingdom,
To order it and establish it with judgment and justice
From that time forward, even forever.
The zeal of the Lord of Hosts will perform this.

(Isaiah 9:6-7)

The Magi came to Jerusalem and asked, "Where is He who has been born King of the Jews? For we have seen His star in the East and have come to worship Him" (Matthew 2:2). They were not of the house of Jacob. They were not even of the house of Jacob's brother, Esau, from whom the paranoid King Herod descended. Yet, they understood that the time for the Great King had come (and that king was not Herod). They had seen His star, which was prophesied in Numbers 24:16-17, "A Star shall come out of Jacob; a Scepter shall rise out of Israel," and they came to give Him honor. These men were of the *goyim*, the surrounding pagan nations—that is, they were Gentiles. The kingdom and the covenant were not theirs, yet they understood that this King would be a blessing to the whole world. For just as the star could be seen in their own land, so the King would arise not only *in* Israel but also *out of* Israel—for the sake of the whole world.

This theme of kingship carried forth throughout the life and ministry of Jesus. After He was baptized by John and driven into the wilderness by the Holy Spirit, where He was tested and proved for forty days, He returned preaching, "The time is fulfilled, the kingdom of God is at hand. Repent and believe in the gospel" (Mark 1:15). His many healing miracles continually manifested the authority of this kingdom: "If I cast out demons by the Spirit of God, surely the kingdom of God has come upon you," He said (Matthew 12:28).

Standing before Pilate, who asked, "Are You the King of the Jews?" Jesus answered, "It is as you say." Before Caiaphas, the high priest who demanded, "Tell us if You are the Christ, the Son of God," Jesus said, "It is as you said. Nevertheless, I say to you, hereafter you will see the Son of Man sitting at the right hand of the Power, and coming on the clouds of heaven" (Matthew 26:64). This was a reference to the prophetic vision of Daniel:

I was watching in the night visions,
And behold, One like the Son of Man,
Coming with the clouds of heaven!
He came to the Ancient of Days,
And they brought Him near before Him.
Then to Him was given dominion and glory and a kingdom,
That all peoples, nations, and languages should serve Him.
His dominion is an everlasting dominion,
Which shall not pass away,
And His kingdom the one
Which shall not be destroyed.

(Daniel 7:13-14)

When He was crucified, the charge fastened above His head read, "This is Jesus the King of the Jews." The resurrection from the dead by the Spirit of God demonstrated that King Jesus the Messiah, born of the seed of David, is indeed the Son of God (Romans 1:4-5). And before He ascended to His throne in heaven, at the right hand of the Father, Jesus came to the disciples and said, "All authority has been given to Me in heaven and on earth"—a powerful statement of His dominion over all (Matthew 28:18).

In Revelation, He is called "King of the Saints" and *Pantokrator*, which means "almighty" or "all-powerful." And of Him, the victorious saints in the book of Revelation sing,

Who shall not fear You, O Lord, and glorify Your name?
For You alone are holy.
For all nations shall come and worship before You,
For Your judgments have been manifested.

(Revelation 15:3-4)

The coming of Jesus the Messiah into the world is the advent of the King who reigns over all.

Displacing Kings

The coming of Jesus the Messiah into the world does not just add another king into the mix. No, He is *the* King, whose kingdom displaces all other kingdoms.

> *Now after Jesus was born in Bethlehem of Judea in the days of Herod the king, behold, wise men from the East came to Jerusalem, saying, "Where is He who has been born King of the Jews? For we have seen His star in the East and have come to worship Him." (Matthew 2:1-2)*

King of the Jews? Herod was under the impression that the Jews already had a king—Herod! He had worked hard to win that appointment from Rome, and he had already killed two of his own sons to protect it. Now come these foreigners looking for a king who was *not* him. He was not happy about that.

The Jews had been looking for the king God promised David centuries earlier, the king who would rule over Israel and subdue all her enemies, the king who would reveal the rule and reign of God throughout the world. Not *a* king but *the* King. With each successor to the throne of David, the Jews hoped that this would be the one. But they were always soon disappointed.

Now they had Herod, an Idumean whose family had been converted to Judaism, and who was selected by the Roman senate to be "King of the Jews." His rule, which began about 40 bc, lasted for 36 years, until his death in 4 BC, not long after Jesus was born. Though he had built many cities and magnificently reconstructed the temple in Jerusalem, he was not well-liked among the Jews. The Sanhedrin condemned his brutal ways, the Sadducees did not care for the way he ruled, the Pharisees hated the way he lived, and the Zealots wanted to kill him. Not to mention the general public, which was heavily taxed to support all his building projects (these many projects are why he is called Herod *the Great*).

So Herod was very paranoid. But the wise men, being out-of-towners, asked where they might find the King of the Jews. Not Herod, of course, but the newborn King, the one promised long ago, whose coming would put Herod out of his place. *Faux pas?*

Herod obliged them. Not because he was a naturally accommodating sort of guy but because he wanted to find this King himself and put an end to him. So he asked the chief priests and scribes where Messiah was to be born. "In Bethlehem of Judea," they said. Herod told the wise men and sent them on with instruction to return when they found the Child, so he could worship Him also. *Liar*!

As the wise men approached Bethlehem, they saw the star again, the one that had alerted them to the birth of the Messiah King, and they rejoiced. After finding and honoring the newborn King, they were wise to Herod's deceit, having been warned in a divine dream not to return to him, and they went back by another way to their own land.

The coming of King Jesus the Messiah into the world displaced Herod as King of the Jews. That is not all, however, for Messiah comes as King over all the nations of the earth—He displaces *every* king. The prophet Zechariah spoke of what His coming would mean, not just for Israel and the Jews, but for the whole world.

And the LORD *shall be King over all the earth. In that day it shall be*—"*The* LORD *is one, and His name one.*" *(Zechariah 14:9)*

The announcement of the gospel is the good news that the King has come into the world, and with Him, the kingdom, the rule and reign of God over all the earth. That is how the apostle Paul understood it.

> *Paul, a bondservant of Jesus Christ, called to be an apostle, separated to the gospel of God which He promised before through His prophets in the Holy Scriptures, concerning His Son Jesus Christ our Lord, who was born of the seed of David according to the flesh, and declared to be the Son of God with power according to the Spirit of holiness, by the resurrection from the dead. Through Him we have received grace and apostleship for obedience to the faith among all nations for His name. (Romans 1:1-5)*

The faith to which all nations are called to be obedient is the truth that Jesus the Messiah, born to the throne of David and declared to be the Son of God by the resurrection from the dead, is *Lord*. This term, "Lord," is not just some religious expression, as it often seems to be reduced to today. Jesus is not Lord merely over "spiritual" matters (as if *spiritual* could be separated out of every other aspect of life), but He is Lord over everything in heaven and earth, which is to say, He is King over all! Before He ascended to heaven, to His throne at the right hand of the Father, Jesus announced to the disciples, "All authority has been given to Me in heaven and on earth" (Matthew 28:18). That is the language of kingly dominion.

Jesus is King, and every nation and every ruler on earth must reckon with that truth. Paul said, "If you declare with your mouth, 'Jesus is Lord,' and believe in your heart that God raised him from the dead, you will be saved" (Romans 10:9 *NIV*). That is the central confession of the apostolic Christian faith and it connects back to the obedience to the gospel Paul described in Romans 1:1-5.

Paul was playing with dynamite, preaching a message that was both powerful and subversive. Throughout the Roman Empire in those days the only acceptable confession was "Caesar is Lord." It was the time of the Imperial cult, when emperors were worshipped as gods and each new Caesar was thought to be the son of God and was honored as savior and king of the world. But Paul's declaration of the gospel repudiated this. Caesar is Lord? NO! Jesus is Lord, and God and King over all the earth.

Jesus is far greater than every king, every president, every head of state all put together! For they must all eventually bow their knees before Him and own Him as their Lord and God and King.

Therefore God also has highly exalted Him and given Him the name which is above every name, that at the name of Jesus every knee should bow, of those in heaven, and of those on earth, and of those under the earth, and that every tongue should confess that Jesus Christ is Lord, to the glory of God the Father. (Philippians 2:9-11)

The King has come—and is coming again. His kingdom displaces every other kingdom and every other king. And His rule shall never end.

The Christmas Story is Not Just for Jews

Christmas is a Jewish story. Oh, I know—this time of year, we are used to greeting our Jewish friends with *Happy Hanukkah* and our Gentile or Christian friends with *Merry Christmas!* However, Christmas—the birth of Jesus—is a Jewish story.

Jesus was a Jew and He came to fulfill the story of Israel that God began with Abraham, continued on through to David and down through the generations that went into Babylonian captivity, all the way to the birth of Jesus. He is the Messiah, the Anointed King that God promised would come into the world to deliver His covenant people and through whom all God's promises would be fulfilled.

But as much as the story of Christmas was for the sake of the Jewish people, it was also for the benefit of all the people of the earth. It is significant that Matthew begins the genealogy of Jesus with Abraham, who was not a Jew but a pagan, which is to say, a Gentile. But God chose to make a great nation through Abraham and promised that through him *all* the nations of the earth would be blessed.

Matthew makes an unusual move in his genealogy and refers to four women. Not the ones that might have been expected—Sarah, Rebekah, Leah or Rachel—but four others: Tamar, Rahab, Ruth and Bathsheba. They highlight four irregularities in the line of David, and therefore in the lineage of Jesus, for they were all Gentiles. Tamar and Rahab were Canaanites, Ruth was a Moabite and Matthew refers to Bathsheba as the wife of "Uriah the Hittite" (although perhaps she might actually have been an Israelite, Matthew highlights the Gentile connection of her husband). Yet, in the grace of God, they were all whirled into the humanity of Jesus,

Matthew's account of Jesus coming into the world also includes the wise men who journeyed from the East to see the newborn King of the Jews. We do not really know who they were or where they came from. *The Revelation of the Magi*, an ancient eastern document written in about the third or fourth century AD, identifies them as kings from the "Great East," mystics who prayed in silence and glorified "the holy majesty of the Lord of life." They were not Jews but Gentiles, yet they are given a place of honor in the Holy Scriptures.

So, Matthew begins his telling of the gospel with significant reference to non-Jews and the roles they played in the Christmas story. At the end of the book, we see that the gospel is just as much for them and all the rest of the nations as it is for the Jews. Before Jesus ascended to His throne at the right hand of the Father, He commissioned His followers to take the good news into all the world.

All authority has been given to Me in heaven and on earth. Go therefore and make disciples of all the nations, baptizing them in the name of the Father and of the Son and of the Holy Spirit, teaching them to observe all things that I have commanded you. (Matthew 28:18-20)

Christmas is all about the coming of the Messiah King into the world and it is very much a Jewish story. It is not just for them but for all who believe and follow King Jesus.

Shepherds' Wonder, Angels' Awe

On the night of Jesus' birth, an angel of the Lord appeared to lowly shepherds tending their flocks in a nearby field. The glory of the Lord flooded them with brilliant light. They had never seen anything like this before and it was far beyond anything they could have imagined.
They were terrified.
But then they heard a voice that turned their terror to wonder:

Then the angel said to them, "Do not be afraid, for behold, I bring you good tidings of great joy which will be to all people." (Luke 2:10)

Good tidings! Great joy! And it would be for all people, even those of low estate and low esteem—like the shepherds—because they were the ones to whom it was first being announced. Quite unexpectedly, they now found themselves at what is the hinge point in the history of the world, and the birth of a king was being heralded to them. In a field. At night. By an angel of the Lord.

> *"For there is born to you this day in the city of David a Savior, who is Christ the Lord." (v. 11)*

This was not about just any king, but about *the* King. The Anointed One promised by God through the prophets long ago. The descendent of David who would sit on his throne and reign forever. This was about Christ the Lord—the Messiah King!

> *"And this will be a sign to you: You will find a Babe wrapped in swaddling cloths, lying in a manger." (v. 12)*

Such an exalted King, yet such a humble entrance into His domain. Wrapped in strips of old cloth and cradled in a feeding trough. That would be the sign to the shepherds. Surely they needed that sign or else they would have been looking in all the wrong places and for all the wrong reasons. And expecting to see finery and a royal court in attendance, they might have felt very much out of place.

Now a multitude of the heavenly army appeared, for as marvelous as this news was for shepherds, it was just as wonderful for angels. They could no longer remain silent but began praising God:

> *Glory to God in the highest, and on earth peace, goodwill toward men. (v. 14)*

The angels were well aware of the glory of God that flooded heaven and filled the earth (see Isaiah 6:3), but now they were witnessing the announcement of good news and redemption entering the world. This is something that, as Peter says, the angels of God eagerly desire to look into, stooping down and craning their necks, as it were, to gaze upon this great mystery (1 Peter 1:12). What they had greatly anticipated was now being realized, and they were in awe.

At the birth of Jesus the Messiah King, shepherds trembled in unexpected wonder and angels stooped deeply in awe.

The Pleasure of God

Glory to God in the highest, and on earth peace among those with whom He is pleased!" (Luke 2:14 ESV)

This is the crescendo of the good news the angel of the Lord announced to shepherds on that night when Jesus was born. A multitude of angels now appeared in the heavens with this praise.

- *Glory to God in the highest.* The highest praises heaven can offer belong to God as He brings forth the fulfillment of the promises He made to Abraham, David and the prophets. God's gift of the Messiah King, Jesus, is the greatest revelation of His glory.
- *Peace on earth.* The coming of Jesus into the world brings the *shalom* of God—the peace that comes from God. It is wholeness, restoration, reconciliation, the mending of rifts between God and man, man and fellow man, man and creation.
- *Among those with whom He is pleased.* The coming of Jesus into the world is the pleasure of God revealed.

It is this last point that I want to focus on here. The Greek word for "pleased" is *eudokia*. It is used often in the New Testament to speak of God's pleasure and delight. The angels' announcement meant that God's favor and good will were now being made manifest on the objects of His delight.

What is it that delights God in? Who are those with whom He is pleased, who bring Him pleasure?

First, it is Jesus Himself that pleases God, not only in His divinity (in which the Father has always delighted) but also in His humanity. When Jesus was baptized by John, identifying with repentant sinners whom He came to save, the voice of the Father announced from heaven, "You are My beloved Son; in You I am *well pleased*" (Luke 3:22). It was repeated again at the mount of transfiguration, where Jesus shone in all His glory and the voice of the Father said, "This is My beloved Son in whom I am *well pleased*. Hear Him!" (Matthew 17:5). In both places, the word for "well pleased" is *eudokeo*.

Eudokeo is the word used when Matthew quotes the prophet Isaiah concerning Messiah and which Matthew applies to Jesus: "Behold! My Servant whom I have chosen, My Beloved in whom My soul is *well pleased!* I will put My Spirit upon Him, and He will declare justice to the Gentiles" (Matthew 13:18). *Eudokeo* is also the word used in the LXX, the ancient Greek translation of the Hebrew Scriptures, in Isaiah 42:1, the passage Matthew quotes.

Jesus used this same word when He spoke to His disciples about the kingdom: "Do not fear, little flock, for it is your Father's *good pleasure* to give you the kingdom" (Luke 12:32). And in His prayer of thanksgiving when the disciples returned rejoicing, having healed the sick, expelled demonic spirits and preached the kingdom of God in Jesus' name: "I thank You, Father, Lord of heaven and earth, that You have hidden these things from the wise and prudent and revealed them to babes. Even so, Father, for so it seemed *good* [pleasing] in Your sight" (Luke 10:21). God is very pleased to reveal His kingdom to those who trust Him. It gives Him great pleasure.

Again and again, it is in Jesus Christ that the pleasure of God is revealed. Paul says that God "predestined us to adoption as sons by Jesus Christ to Himself, according to the *good pleasure* of His will … having made known to us the mystery of His will, according to His *good pleasure* which He purposed in Himself" (Ephesians 1:5, 9). "For it *pleased* the Father that in Him [Jesus] all the fullness should dwell, and by Him to reconcile all things to Himself, by Him, whether things on earth or things in heaven, having made peace through the blood of His cross" (Colossians 1:19).

But it is also in *us* that God desires to show His pleasure. Paul says, "It is God who works in you both to will and to do for His *good pleasure*" (Philippians 2:13). In 2 Thessalonians 1:11-12, he says, "Therefore we also pray always for you that our God would count you worthy of this calling, and fulfill all the *good pleasure* of His goodness and the work of faith with power, that the name of our Lord Jesus Christ may be glorified in you, and you in Him, according to the grace of our God and the Lord Jesus Christ."

God is doing a work of faith in us, His power manifesting in us to reveal the glory of King Jesus dwelling within. It is His good pleasure to bring this work to fulfillment in us.

It is by faith that we enter into the richness of God's pleasure. "Without faith it is impossible to *please* Him, for he who comes to God must believe that He is, and that He is a rewarder of those who diligently seek Him" (Hebrews 11:6). The Greek word for "please" here is not *eudokia* but *euarestio*, but it means the same thing. Without faith, it is impossible to please God, but believing God, seeking Him with diligent expectation, pleases God greatly.

Paul tells us, "Faith comes by hearing, and hearing by the Word of God" (Romans 10:17). For, "in the wisdom of God, the world through wisdom did not know God, it *pleased* God through the foolishness of the message preached to save those who believe" (1 Corinthians 1:21). It pleases God for us to believe the good news of Jesus the Messiah and, through faith, bring us to restoration and wholeness in Him.

The coming of King Jesus into the world reveals the glory of God and the peace of God but also the pleasure of God.

The Shepherds' Return

So it was, when the angels had gone away from them into heaven, that the shepherds said to one another, "Let us now go to Bethlehem and see this thing that has come to pass, which the Lord has made known to us." And they came with haste and found Mary and Joseph, and the Babe lying in a manger.

Now when they had seen Him, they made widely known the saying which was told them concerning this Child. And all those who heard it marveled at those things which were told them by the shepherds. But Mary kept all these things and pondered them in her heart. Then the shepherds returned, glorifying and praising God for all the things that they had heard and seen, as it was told them. (Luke 2:15-18)

The angel of the Lord brought the news of the coming of the Messiah King. A multitude of angels filled the sky, releasing the sound of God's glory in the heaven, God's peace on the earth, God's pleasure on His people. Then they returned to heaven.

The shepherds did not waste a moment but immediately set off to Bethlehem to see what the Lord had spoken to them by the angels. "Let us go *now*," they said, and they "came *with haste.*" What they saw was just as it had been told them by the angel. Here was the Babe, the long promised Messiah, lying in a manger. They did not pause over the incongruity of a great King born in a lowly stable and placed in the feeding trough of animals. Had not the appearance of heaven's angels to lowly shepherds been equally unexpected? But the strangeness of these things did not take away one bit from the truth of what they now witnessed for themselves.

Seeing the Child, they began telling everyone they could find all they had heard and seen. How could they refrain—it was so amazing. Everyone wondered at the joyful news. Even Mary treasured it all up in her heart.

Then the shepherds returned to their fields, but they were not as they were before. How could they be? Having heard the angelic message, the sound of heaven on earth, and seen for themselves the infant Messiah King, and shared the news with everyone they met, they were changed. They returned full of praise, giving God glory.

What have you heard? What have you seen? Who are you telling? What is your joy? And how have you been changed?

Simeon and Anna in Expectation

Behold, there was a man in Jerusalem whose name was Simeon, and this man was just and devout, waiting for the Consolation of Israel, and the Holy Spirit was upon him. And it had been revealed to him by the Holy Spirit that he would not see death before he had seen the Lord's Christ. (Luke 2:25-26)

Forty days after Jesus was born, Mary and Joseph brought him to Jerusalem, to the temple to be dedicated to the Lord (Luke 2:22-24). This was standard practice for all firstborn children, according to the Law of Moses. There was nothing unusual about what they were doing, except for what happened next.

It is at this point in his narrative that Luke introduces us to Simeon, and in a very significant way—with the word *Behold*. In the Bible, "behold" is a word that focuses our attention and calls us to see something of importance. Others in the temple that day might not have noticed what happened next, but Luke does not want us to miss it.

Simeon was a man of no special prominence in Jerusalem. Neither a priest, nor a politician, nor a religious leader. But he was a man who had received a very special promise from God, revealed to him by the Holy Spirit: Before he died, Simeon would lay his eyes on God's Messiah.

Now, on the very same day that Mary and Joseph brought Jesus into the temple, the Holy Spirit led Simeon in also. "By the Spirit," is how Luke puts it. We do not know exactly how it was, whether it was a conscious revelation or merely a prompting in Simeon's spirit to which he had learned to be obedient. However it happened, the Spirit of God got him there at exactly the right place and precisely the right time.

It was a moment of singular fulfillment for Simeon, certainly, but more importantly, it was a realization of God's plan from the beginning. His purpose in Adam, in Abraham, in Jacob, in Moses and the children of Israel, in King David and all the prophets, was now being realized in the presentation of Jesus. Simeon immediately recognized Him for who He was—the Messiah, God's Anointed. Scooping Him up in his arms, Simeon blessed God:

> *Lord, now You are letting Your servant depart in peace,*
> *According to Your word;*
> *For my eyes have seen Your salvation*
> *Which You have prepared before the face of all peoples,*
> *A light to bring revelation to the Gentiles,*
> *And the glory of Your people Israel."*
>
> *(Luke 2:29-32)*

Now, coming into the temple at that exact same moment was a very elderly prophetess named Anna. She had been a widow for about 84 years and had spent her life fasting and praying, night and day, in the temple courts (vv. 36-37). Perhaps she had seen Simeon before. Perhaps they had spoken about the promise he had received. Or perhaps it was a life spent in prayer which had sharpened her spiritual senses so that, when she saw Simeon with Mary and Joseph and Jesus, she immediately understood what was happening. Though Luke does not say, there is no reason to doubt that she, too, was led in by the Spirit. Recognizing the presence of Jesus, her response was simple, but significant. "She gave thanks to the Lord, and spoke of Him to all those who looked for redemption in Jerusalem" (v. 38).

You see, like Simeon, Anna had an expectation that the Anointed One would soon come and God's promise would be fulfilled. And they were not the only ones. There were others also who had such an expectation and "looked for redemption in Jerusalem." Anna sought them out and shared the good news with them.

Of course, Anna and Simeon were old and would not get to see Jesus move through the stages in His life. Nor would they experience the bewilderment of the cross—or see Him in the glory of His resurrection. No matter. They had learned to hear the voice of God and to be led by the Spirit. They had learned to live in expectation of the promise of God. They had learned to behold, and to understand what they were seeing. They had seen enough to know that God's kingdom purpose in Israel would be fulfilled and all the world would be blessed by it. It was now beginning before their eyes.

Two thousand years later, we have still not yet seen the full manifestation God's kingdom in the world, the will of God being done thoroughly and completely on earth as it is in heaven. But it *has* begun and is increasing every day. Jesus said, "From the days of John the Baptist until now, the kingdom of heaven has been forcefully advancing and forceful men lay hold of it" (Matthew 11:12 *NIV*). "The law and the prophets were until John. Since that time the kingdom of God has been preached, and everyone is pressing into it" (Luke 16:16). The apostle John put it this way: "The darkness is passing away, and the true light is already shining" (1 John 2:8).

The infant Messiah, beheld and blessed by Simeon and Anna, grew to manhood and went to the cross for the sake of the world. Forty days after His resurrection, He ascended to His throne at the right hand of the Father. We are now living in the days of King Jesus the Messiah, Lord of heaven and earth, of whom the prophet Isaiah said, "Of the increase of His government and peace there will be no end" (Isaiah 9:7).

As you look to a new year, do you hear the promise of God? Do you see the kingdom of God breaking into the world and increasing? Do you behold King Jesus? Do you pray as He taught, "Kingdom of God, come. Will of God, be done on earth as it is in heaven"? Do you yield yourself to be led by the Spirit of God, that this expectation may come to pass in you?

He Appeared in the Flesh

Beyond all question, the mystery from which true godliness springs is great: He appeared in the flesh, was vindicated by the Spirit, was seen by angels, was preached among the nations, was believed on in the world, was taken up in glory. (1 Timothy 3:16 NIV)

What Paul tells us here is something he describes as "beyond all question," or, "without controversy" (*NKJV*). The Greek word is *homologoumenos*, which has to do with confession. Paul is saying something about which the early Church was quite in agreement, a confession of faith, straight up and orthodox. He is likely quoting a creed or hymn that was already in circulation in the Church.

It is a "mystery," Paul says. In the Bible, a mystery is not a secret but a revelation, something that God has made known in Jesus Christ. It is not something we could ever have reasoned our way to, nor is it an invention dreamed up by men. It must be revealed to us by God and is therefore a matter of His grace. And so it is with the "mystery of godliness."

Godliness is holiness, or piety, or the "fear of the Lord." Godliness is *God-centeredness*. It is about what it means to be in proper relationship with God.

In the words of the *NIV*, Paul calls this "the mystery from which true godliness springs." It is about how God has reconciled the world and all things in heaven and on earth to Himself through the Lord Jesus Christ.

Now all things are of God, who has reconciled us to Himself through Jesus Christ, and has given us the ministry of reconciliation, that is,

> *that God was in Christ reconciling the world to Himself, not imputing their trespasses to them, and has committed to us the word of reconciliation. (2 Corinthians 5:18-19)*

> *For it pleased the Father that in Him all the fullness should dwell, and by Him to reconcile all things to Himself, by Him, whether things on earth or things in heaven, having made peace through the blood of His cross. (Colossians 1:19-20)*

This mystery about which Paul speaks is, in other words, a confession of the gospel, the proclamation of the good news about Jesus the Messiah, encapsulated in six short statements. It begins with a statement about the incarnation, for it is to the Lord Jesus in His humanity that the rest of the statements of this confession apply:

- *"He appeared in the flesh."* This is where the mystery begins. It is the mystery of the Incarnation, the revelation of God in human flesh. "The Word became flesh and dwelt among us, and we beheld His glory, the glory as of the only begotten of the Father, full of grace and truth" (John 1:14).
- *"Was vindicated by the Spirit."* Though He was in manifested in the flesh, the Lord Jesus was vindicated in the Spirit. He was anointed with the Holy Spirit (Luke 4:17-21; Acts 10:38). Paul opens his letter to the Romans with this twofold mystery of flesh and spirit: "Concerning His Son Jesus Christ our Lord, who was born of the seed of David according to the flesh, and declared to be the Son of God with power according to the Spirit of Holiness, by the resurrection from the dead" (Romans 1:3-4).
- *"Was seen by angels."* Angels attended and announced both the

incarnation and the resurrection of Jesus. They were present to minister to Jesus after the temptation in the wilderness. The author of Hebrews demonstrates the superiority of Jesus, Son of God, over the angels of God. Angels are not to be worshipped as some false teachers taught (this was one of the errors Paul addressed in his letter to the Colossians). Rather, Jesus is worshipped by the angels. When He ascended to the throne of heaven, angels surrounded Him. Peter said that the angels greatly desire to look into the mystery of the gospel, the Christian faith (1 Peter 1:12).

- *"Was preached among the nations."* The coming of Jesus the Messiah was not just for the Jews, but for the whole world—every tribe, every tongue, every ethnic group—the nations. Peter learned the depth of this mystery in Acts 10, when He was sent to Cornelius, a Roman who reverenced the God of the Jews. Paul understood His own calling to be especially to the non-Jews, apostle to the nations.

- *"Was believed on in the world."* These mysteries of the Spirit are very improbable to our natural perceptions, which have been turned upside down by the deceptions of the evil one and the bondage of sin. And yet, Light entered the world and blind eyes have been enabled to see by the proclaiming of the mystery, the preaching of the Gospel. "Faith comes by hearing," Paul says, "and hearing by the Word of God" (Romans 10:17).

- *"Was taken up in glory."* Forty days after His resurrection, the Lord Jesus ascended into heaven and was received up into glory, where He is enthroned at the right hand of the Father. The kingdom of God has broken into the world, and the King has taken His rightful place on the throne of heaven to reign in glory forever as Lord of heaven and earth. Paul tells us that every believer in King Jesus the Messiah is now seated together with Him in that heavenly dimension (Ephesians 2:6).

The mystery begins with the incarnation, God in the flesh, and climaxes with the exaltation of Jesus the Messiah in highest glory. Elsewhere, in his letter to the Jesus followers at Philippi, Paul speaks of the mystery of incarnation and exaltation in this way:

> *Let this mind be in you which was also in Christ Jesus, who, being in the form of God, did not consider it robbery to be equal with God, but made Himself of no reputation, taking the form of a bondservant, and coming in the likeness of men. And being found in appearance as a man, He humbled Himself and became obedient to the point of death, even the death of the cross. Therefore God also has highly exalted Him and given Him the name which is above every name, that at the name of Jesus every knee should bow, of those in heaven, and of those on earth, and of those under the earth, and that every tongue should confess that Jesus Christ is Lord, to the glory of God the Father. (Philippians 2:5-11).*

So the great mystery is also a paradox, for it turns out that *God-*centeredness is gloriously centered on a *man*—Jesus the Messiah, God become flesh. He is the one we believe and confess, and in Him we learn true godliness.

The Shekinah Dwelling (Part 1)

And the Word became flesh and dwelt among us, and we beheld His glory, the glory as of the only begotten of the Father, full of grace and truth. (John 1:14)

The Greek verb for "dwell" is *skenoo* and means to tent or encamp. The noun form is *skenos*, which refers to a tent or tabernacle. In the Septuagint (or LXX), which is an ancient Greek translation of the Hebrew Old Testament, *skenos* is used to translate the Hebrew word for "tabernacle," which is *mishkan*. *Mishkan* is from the Hebrew verb *shakan*, which means to dwell or inhabit.

The Hebrew root for *mishkan* are the three Hebrew consonants *shin, kaf, nun* . Note how similar these are to the consonants in *skenos* (the s-k-n sound). This may be an indication that the Greeks borrowed the Hebrew word *shakan* and transliterated it into *skenos*.

Not to overburden you with too many ancient and foreign terms, but I would like to talk to you about *Shekinah*. It is from the same root as *mishkan* and *shakan* and speaks of dwelling, resting, abiding, and even of nesting. In ancient Jewish writings, it is used of the divine presence, the manifestation of the glory of God. In the Old Testament, the tabernacle (*mishkan*) was the place God chose to reveal His presence in a special way to His people. The Targums, ancient translations of the Old Testament from Hebrew into its cousin language, Aramaic, speak of God's manifest presence as the *"shekinah* of His glory."

In the Bible, the tabernacle was the place of God's divine presence, the place where He manifested His glory. This manifestation was the

Shekinah, the divine glory resting and abiding with His people.

The Gospel of John says, "And the Word became flesh and dwelt among us." John is speaking of Jesus as the Word (*Logos*, the Greek word for "word"), which was consistent with the Jewish practice of referring to God by the Hebrew and Aramaic equivalents for "word," because God revealed Himself by His Word. And that is the point John makes: God has now revealed Himself in human flesh as Jesus, the Word who was with Him from the beginning and, indeed, is God (John 1:1-2). He is that Word by which God created the heavens and the earth, the Word by whom all things were spoken into existence.

This same Word became flesh—*incarnation* is the theological term—and dwelt among us, *tabernacled* among us, manifesting the presence of God among us. "And we beheld His glory," John says, and the Jews of his day would have understood this as the *Shekinah*. The divine glory revealed uniquely in Jesus is "the glory as of the only begotten of the Father."

This *Shekinah* glory, John says, was "full of grace and truth." In the Old Testament, the combination of "grace" and "truth", or rather, the Hebrew equivalents, *hesed* and *emeth*, spoke of God Himself. *Hesed* is the word by which God was revealed in His mercy and kindness. *Emeth* revealed Him in His faithfulness and truth. The word "full" indicates completeness, leaving nothing lacking. "For in Him [Jesus] dwells *all the fullness* of the Godhead bodily" (Colossians 2:9).

Jesus is the Living Tabernacle, where the presence of God is fully manifested among His people. His glory, the *Shekinah* glory, fully reveals the faithful love and mercy of God.

The Shekinah Dwelling (Part 2)

To them God willed to make known what are the riches of the glory of this mystery among the Gentiles: which is Christ in you, the hope of glory. (Colossians 1:27)

King Jesus the Messiah is the Word who became flesh and tabernacled among us, manifesting the divine presence, the dwelling place of the *Shekinah* glory of God. Since then, He has ascended, in His body, to the right hand of the Father, where He now rules over heaven and earth forever. But what of the *Shekinah*, the glory of the divine presence?

In the Old Testament, the dwelling place God chose to manifest His presence was the tabernacle in the wilderness, then the tent of David, and finally, the temple in Jerusalem. With the sacrifice of Messiah Jesus for our sins, the temple system of burnt offerings and sacrifices, which served as a type or foreshadow, was fulfilled, and the old handmade temple was rendered obsolete. This was one of the points the author of Hebrews emphasized:

The Holy Spirit indicating this, that the way into the Holiest of All was not yet made manifest while the first tabernacle was still standing … But Christ came as High Priest of the good things to come, with the greater and more perfect tabernacle not made with hands, that is, not of this creation. (Hebrews 9:8, 11)

Jesus came as the mediator of a new covenant, the one foretold by Jeremiah and Ezekiel (see Jeremiah 31:31-33 and Ezekiel 36:25-27), in which God would write His law upon our hearts and place His Spirit within us. This required a temple that was *not* made with human hands.

But God has not left Himself without a place to manifest His presence, His *Shekinah*, on earth. The apostles teach us that there remains yet a temple on earth, a dwelling place where God has chosen to reveal His glory. It is not a temple of wood and stone, but a temple made without hands. It is the people of God themselves. The apostle Paul says,

> *Do you not know that you are the temple of God and that the Spirit of God dwells in you? If anyone defiles the temple of God, God will destroy him. For the temple of God is holy, which temple you are. (1 Corinthians 3:16-17)*

Again, Paul says, quoting Ezekiel,

> *For you are the temple of the living God. As God has said: "I will dwell in them and walk among them. I will be their God, and they shall be My people." (2 Corinthians 6:16)*

Those who have received King Jesus the Messiah are now the temple of God, because He has placed His Spirit in us, just as He promised in Ezekiel. Collectively, as a people, we are the place where God dwells on earth. But also individually, we are, each one, the temple of God. He dwells in our bodies as well as our spirits:

> *Or do you not know that your body is the temple of the Holy Spirit who is in you, whom you have from God, and you are not your own? For you were bought at a price; therefore glorify God in your body and in your spirit, which are God's. (1 Corinthians 6:19-20)*

The apostle Peter likewise understood his own body to be a tabernacle, or tent.

> *Yes, I think it is right, as long as I am in this tent, to stir you up by reminding you, knowing that shortly I must put off my tent, just as our Lord Jesus Christ showed me.* (2 Peter 1:13-14)

The Greek word for "tent" here is *skenoma*, which is used of the divine dwelling. And that is likely how Peter would be thinking of it here, fully aware, as he wrote just a few verses earlier, of the "exceedingly great and precious promises" God has given us and that those who belong to Jesus the Messiah have become "partakers of the divine nature" (2 Peter 1:3-4).

God's promise of a new covenant and a new temple was not just for the Jews but also for all the nations. In his letter to the Church at Ephesus, Paul speaks to both the Jewish and Gentile believers in Jesus:

> *Now, therefore, you are no longer strangers and foreigners, but fellow citizens with the saints and members of the household of God, having been built on the foundation of the apostles and prophets, Jesus Christ Himself being the chief cornerstone, in whom the whole building, being fitted together, grows into a holy temple in the Lord, in whom you also are being built together for a dwelling place of God in the Spirit.* (Ephesians 2:19-22)

Paul makes the point again in Colossians: Jesus the Messiah comes to dwell in believing Gentiles as well as in believing Jews.

> *To them God willed to make known what are the riches of the glory of this mystery among the Gentiles: which is Christ in you, the hope of glory.* (Colossians 1:27)

Messiah—God, the Word that became flesh and dwelt *among* us—now dwells *in* us. Paul calls it "the hope of glory." Surely, the glory of God's presence dwelling in us is the *Shekinah*. Because King Jesus the Messiah dwells in us by His Spirit, we can expect the *Shekinah* glory of God to be made known *in* us and *to* us and *through* us.

A Tabernacle for the Nations

My tabernacle also shall be with them; indeed I will be their God, and they shall be My people. The nations also will know that I, the LORD, sanctify Israel, when My sanctuary is in their midst forevermore. (Ezekiel 37:27-28)

This is a promise God made to Israel in one of her darkest hours, when she was divided and taken into captivity because of her idolatry. There would be a return, a restoration, a rebirth. The past would be past and God would create a new relationship with her.

David My servant shall be king over them, and they shall all have one shepherd; they shall also walk in My judgments and observe My statutes, and do them. Then they shall dwell in the land that I have given to Jacob My servant, where your fathers dwelt; and they shall dwell there, they, their children, and their children's children, forever; and My servant David shall be their prince forever. Moreover I will make a covenant of peace with them, and it shall be an everlasting covenant with them; I will establish them and multiply them, and I will set My sanctuary in their midst forevermore. My tabernacle also shall be with them; indeed I will be their God, and they shall be My people. (Ezekiel 37:24-27)

"David" would be king over them. Of course, David was long dead by this time, but the reference here is to the *Son* of David, that is, to the "Anointed One" God promised would reign on the throne over Israel. As David was literally a shepherd, so this royal descendent would also be a Shepherd over them. There would be a return to the land where they would dwell forever. God would make a new covenant with them, a covenant of peace—*shalom*, the wholeness that comes from God—and it would be eternal. God would establish His sanctuary, His holiness, among them. His tabernacle, His divine dwelling place, would be with them and they would be His holy people, set apart for His pleasure and purpose. They would enjoy special relationship with God, fellowship with the Divine.

This promise is fulfilled in Jesus the Messiah, the Son of David, who is called the Good Shepherd. He is the mediator of a new and better covenant, which is established on better promises (Hebrew 8:6). He is not only the High Priest of that covenant; He is the sacrifice upon which it was based. On the night before He was crucified, He blessed the bread of the Passover table and gave it to the disciples: "This is My body which is given for you." Then He took the cup and said, "This cup is the new covenant in My blood, which is shed for you" (Luke 22:19-20).

Jesus is the tabernacle of God. He is the Word who "became flesh and dwelt among us" (John 1:14). The Greek word for "dwelt" (*skenoo*) relates linguistically to the Hebrew word for "tabernacle" (*mishkan*). The Word became flesh and "tabernacled" among us.

"The nations also will know that I, the LORD, sanctify Israel, when My sanctuary is in their midst forevermore," God said. This promise was for Israel and the land God gave to Jacob, but it would be a witness to all the nations of the world that God has created a people on earth and dwells among them. Indeed, the promise was for the sake *of the nations,* for God created Israel to be not only a holy nation but also a "kingdom of priests" (Exodus 19:6). That is, they were to bring the blessing and promise of God to all the nations.

We find this fulfilled in the New Testament. Before He ascended to His throne at the right hand of the Father, Jesus gathered the disciples together and announced, "All authority has been given to Me in heaven and on earth. Go therefore and make disciples of all the nations, baptizing them in the name of the Father and of the Son and of the Holy Spirit, teaching them to observe all things that I have commanded you; and lo, I am with you always, even to the end of the age" (Matthew 28:18-20). This was no longer just about the little piece of ground in the Middle East that God gave to Jacob, for Paul tells us that Abraham became heir to the *whole world* (Romans 4:13).

So, it was not just for ethnic Israel but *all* the nations were to be discipled and baptized and instructed. This does not mean, however, that the nations would receive the promise *in addition to* or *apart from* Israel—and certainly not *instead of* Israel. But, in Paul's metaphor, in Romans 11, they are "grafted" into the root stock that is Israel, to be partakers of the blessing and promise of God as part of Israel (Romans 11:16-24).

The tabernacle of God, Jesus the Messiah, has come to abide all over the world, in every nation. All who believe Him receive the promise and become part of the sanctuary, the holy people with whom and in whom God dwells. And all the nations will know.

Let Earth Receive Her King

Psalm 98 is gospel-shaped. That is, although it has its own historical setting in the story of Israel, it finds its greatest fulfillment in the gospel—the good news about the kingdom of God and of Jesus, God's anointed King.

Sing to the Lord a new song, for he has done marvelous things!
His right hand and his holy arm have worked salvation for him.
(Psalm 98:1)

The gospel is not just *a* new song but *the* new song, the fulfillment of God's promises to Israel. Jesus began His ministry by announcing the gospel: "The time is fulfilled, and the kingdom of God is at hand. Repent, and believe in the gospel" (Mark 1:15). The gospel is the ultimate expression of God's purpose for the world, from beginning to end: "God, who at various times and in various ways spoke in time past to the fathers by the prophets, has in these last days spoken to us by His Son, whom He has appointed heir of all things, through whom also He made the worlds; who being the brightness of His glory and the express image of His person, and upholding all things by the word of His power, when He had by Himself purged our sins, sat down at the right hand of the Majesty on high" (Hebrews 1:1-2).

The LORD has made known His salvation;
His righteousness He has revealed in the sight of the nations.

> *He has remembered His mercy and His faithfulness*
> *to the house of Israel;*
> *All the ends of the earth have seen the salvation of our God.*
>
> *(Psalm 98:2-3)*

In the gospel, God has brought His salvation into the world not only for Israel's sake but for all the nations of the earth. That is why, after the resurrection but before He ascended to His throne at the right hand of the Father, Jesus said to His disciples, "All authority has been given to Me in heaven and on earth. Go therefore and make disciples of all the nations" (Matthew 28:18-19). And the apostle Paul, even as he was under house arrest in Rome, teaching and testifying about the kingdom of God, said, "Therefore let it be known to you that the salvation of God has been sent to the Gentiles [Greek, *ethnos*, nations], and they will hear it!" (Acts 28:23-28). Add to this the intriguing fact that the Hebrew word for "salvation" in Psalm 98:2-3 is *yeshuah*, which in name form is *Yeshua*, the Hebrew name for Jesus, and it is reason for the whole world to rejoice:

> *Shout joyfully to the LORD, all the earth;*
> *Break forth in song, rejoice, and sing praises.*
> *Sing to the LORD with the harp,*
> *With the harp and the sound of a psalm,*
> *With trumpets and the sound of a horn;*
> *Shout joyfully before the LORD, the King.*
> *Let the sea roar, and all its fullness,*
> *The world and those who dwell in it;*
> *Let the rivers clap their hands;*
> *Let the hills be joyful together before the LORD.*
>
> *(Psalm 98:4-8)*

In announcing the good news about King Jesus the Messiah, God has revealed His salvation to the nations. It is cause for celebrating with shouts of joy and loud praises to God. Even creation itself is depicted as getting in on the act—the seas roar, the rivers "clap their hands," the hills are full of joy—because its own redemption is at hand. "For the earnest expectation of the creation eagerly waits for the revealing of the sons of God. For the creation was subjected to futility, not willingly, but because of Him who subjected it in hope; because the creation itself also will be delivered from the bondage of corruption into the glorious liberty of the children of God" (Romans 8:19-21).

For He is coming to judge the earth.
With righteousness He shall judge the world,
And the peoples with equity.

(Psalm 98:9)

The Lord Jesus has ascended to His throne at the right hand of the Father, where He rules and reigns with all authority over heaven and earth. But there is coming a day when He will return to judge the world. Paul spoke of that day in his sermon to the philosophers on Mars Hill, in Athens. He proclaimed to them the God they did not know, that He has "appointed a day on which He will judge the world in righteousness by the Man [Jesus the Messiah] whom He has ordained. He has given assurance of this to all by raising Him from the dead" (Acts 17:31).

Often, when people think of God judging the world, they imagine a hail of fire and brimstone raining down and leaving behind a scene of death and desolation. In that portrayal, God judging the world means God destroying the world.

Not so. As we saw above, creation is not waiting to be destroyed and put out of its misery. It is waiting to be delivered, set free from the bondage of corruption, to experience the glory and freedom of the redeemed as God brings His plan to completion. When King Jesus comes to judge the world, it is make everything in the world the way it was always meant to be. His righteousness, which is to say, His rightness, sets everything right. "Behold, I make all things new," are His words at the end of the New Testament (Revelation 21:5).

That is the joyful anticipation of the gospel. The kingdom of God has come into the world, with Jesus as God's anointed King. And when He returns the kingdom will be found in completeness—heaven on earth—the will of God being done on earth just as it is in heaven. Let all the earth come and sing and shout for joy because of this good news.

Psalm 98, then, is most appropriate as we consider Christmas and the advent of the kingdom of God. "This psalm," said Saint Athanasius, "tells of the Lord's first coming and that people of all nations will believe in Him." Isaac Watts' famous "Joy to the World"—usually reserved for Christmastime, but actually very fitting throughout the year—is based on this psalm.

Joy to the World

Joy to the world! The Lord is come
Let earth receive her King!
Let every heart prepare Him room
And heaven and nature sing

Joy to the world! The Savior reigns
Let men their songs employ
While fields and floods, rocks, hills and plains
Repeat the sounding joy

No more let sins and sorrows grow
Nor thorns infest the ground
He comes to make His blessings flow
Far as the curse is found

He rules the world with truth and grace
And makes the nations prove
The glories of His righteousness
And wonders of His love

Also by Jeff Doles

He Come from the Glory
A Walking Barefoot Christmas

Available in CD and MP3
Listen to audio clips and order at
www.walkingbarefoot.com

Also by Jeff Doles

There is Always Joy!
Paul's Letter to the Jesus Believers at Philippi
Bite-Sized Studies Through the Book of Philippians

5.5 x 8.5 in., 125 pages

Available at www.walkingbarefoot.com

Also by Jeff Doles

The Focus of Our Faith
Paul's Letter to the Jesus Believers at Colosse
Bite-Sized Studies Through the Book of Colossians

5.5 x 8.5 in., 151 pages

Available at www.walkingbarefoot.com

Also by Jeff Doles

Keeping the Faith When Things Get Tough
Peter's Letter to Jesus Believers Scattered Everywhere
Bite-Sized Studies Through the Book of First Peter

5.5 x 8.5 in., 93 pages

Available at www.walkingbarefoot.com

Also by Jeff Doles

The Kingdom of Heaven on Earth
Keys to the Kingdom of God
in the Gospel of Matthew

6 x 9 in., 194 pages

Available at www.walkingbarefoot.com

Also by Jeff Doles

God's Word in *Your* Mouth
Changing Your World Through Faith

6 x 9 in., 140 pages

Available at www.walkingbarefoot.com

Also by Jeff Doles

Walking Barefoot
Living in Prayer, Faith and the Power of God

6 x 9 in., 140 pages

Available at www.walkingbarefoot.com

Also by Jeff Doles

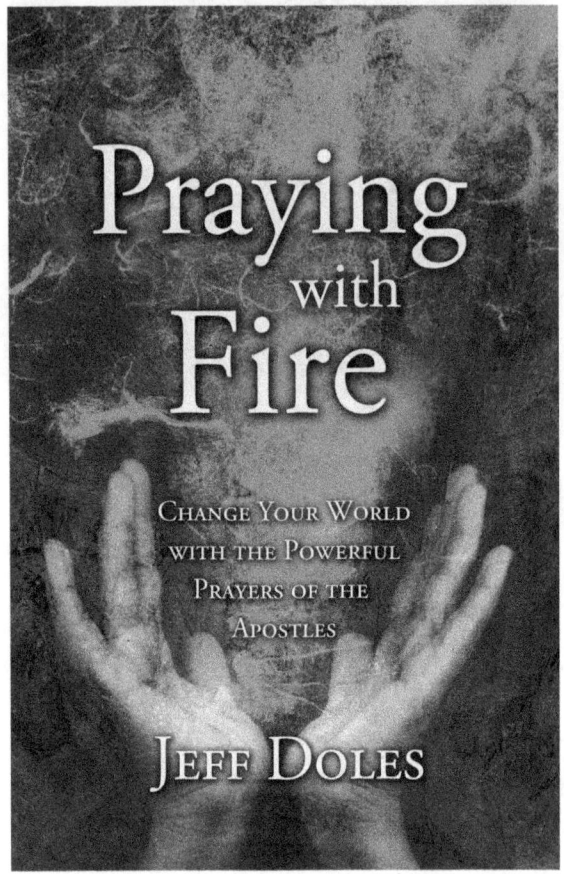

Praying With Fire
**Change Your World with the
Powerful Prayers of the Apostles**

6 x 9 in., 104 pages

Available at www.walkingbarefoot.com

Also by Jeff Doles

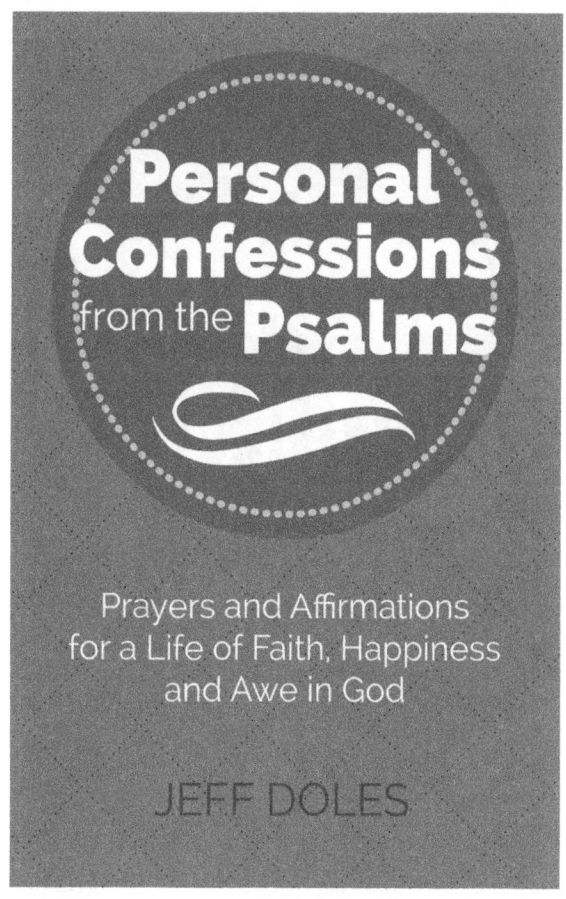

**Personal Confessions
from the Psalms**
Prayers and Affirmations for a Life of Faith,
Happiness and Awe in God

5.5 x 8.5 in., 98 pages

Available at www.walkingbarefoot.com

Also by Jeff Doles

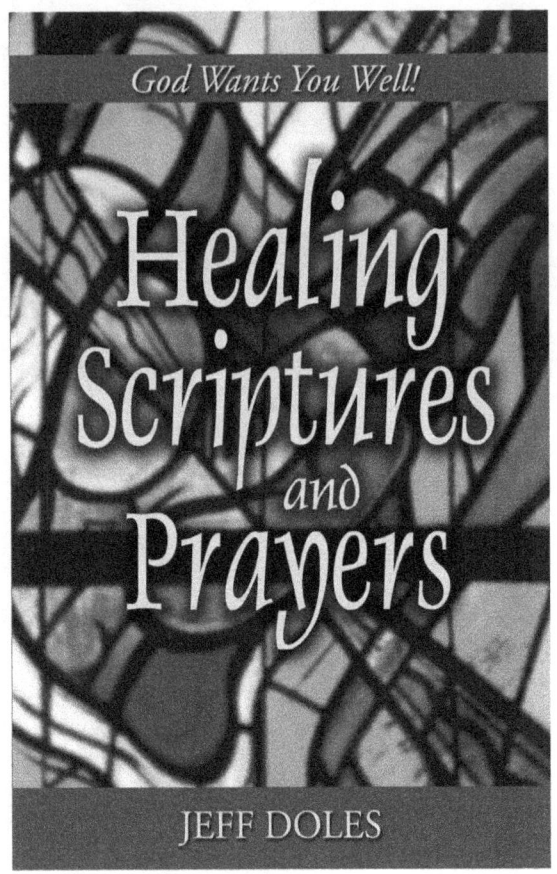

Healing Scriptures and Prayers

6 x 9 in., 120 pages

Available at www.walkingbarefoot.com

Soak in the Healing Scriptures

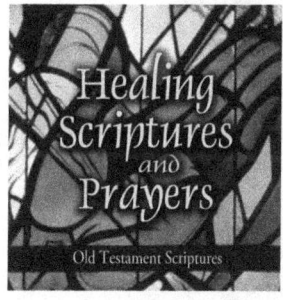

Vol. 1: Old Testament Scriptures

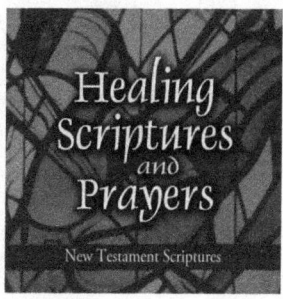

Vol. 2: New Testament Scriptures

Vol. 3: Healing Names of God

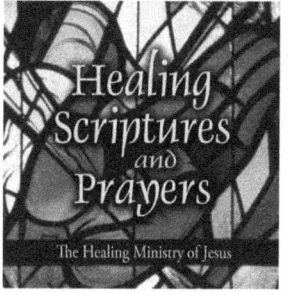

Vol. 4: The Healing Ministry of Jesus

Healing Scriptures and Prayers

Available in CD and MP3
Listen to audio clips and order at
www.walkingbarefoot.com

Also by Jeff Doles

Miracles and Manifestations of the Holy Spirit in the History of the Church

9.6 x 7.4 in., 274 pages

Available at www.walkingbarefoot.com

Also by Jeff Doles

On This Pilgrim's Way
A Walking Barefoot Hymnal

Available in CD and MP3
Listen to audio clips and order at
www.walkingbarefoot.com

www.ingramcontent.com/pod-product-compliance
Lightning Source LLC
Chambersburg PA
CBHW031453040426
42444CB00007B/1075